flush•the•hush

the long
bright cloud
of screaming
rush

Jacques-Pierre Dumas is an aspiring novelist and poet. He holds a deep love of nature and adventure, believing that inspiration is all around us. Originally from South Africa, J.P. resides in Auckland, where he has developed a passion for translingualism, cultural code-mixing, and auditory exploration in poetry.

Molly Joy Henderson is from Auckland. She has studied English and Film at the University of Auckland and is training to become a primary school teacher. She loves poetry, music, and dance and has a passion for feminist, nonsensical, and spoken word poetry.

Chris McMenamin is a poet, librettist, accordionist, and choirmaster from Auckland. Chris enjoys reading metaphysical poetry, and is training to teach Music and English at a secondary level. Current creative projects of his include an opera in three acts and two languages, an Elizabethan comedy, and a Requiem Mass in G minor.

Susannah Whaley is from New Plymouth, Taranaki. She has studied English Literature and Spanish at the University of Auckland and plans to study Honours in English in 2017. She loves learning languages and enjoys poetry and fiction writing. She finds inspiration in simple things.

flush•the•hush

the long
bright cloud
of screaming
rush

Jacques-Pierre Dumas
Molly Joy Henderson
Chris McMenamin
Susannah Whaley

For Michele and Lisa

• thank you for your nurture and guidance •

First published December 2016

for publication information, contact
Chris McMenamin
popmadon@gmail.com

ISBN: 978-0-473-38067-0

Cover and section title pages contain squares from the Resene Paints Ltd. Total Colour System Multi-finish range.

Contents

Wistful™ B73-042-284

Harlequin™ V43-062-324

Tango™ O66-147-058

Cabaret™ R62-100-011

in the lovelight

in the lovelight of the evening
that dusky rosebeam moment
before the sun slips away
but the lamplights are on
and the air is
crisp

I will stop you there
on the sidewalk
and the hot tar
will sink into our toes

and in that moment
I will give you a chocolate box
tied with pink ribbon
containing three chocolates.

and I will say
one is for the light behind us
one is for the melting globe
above our heads
and one
is for the stars
that are yet to bloom in the sky.

and you can choose
if you take them
(and you must take all of them)

but
if you do not
I will leave you on that blank sidewalk
and I will not give you chocolates
any more.

SW

From Grace Nichol's 'Beauty'

Beauty is a

every woman

fat thin smiling

long short hair entwining

forgotten dust of memory

kisses clinging to her cheek

hair bright strands of kaleidoscope here

the sun shines through its peep holes

and falls on her

every skin.

SW

DANCE OF DEATH AND LOVE; AND KING

Death; plain, simple Death,
I have not known Thy tiresome sting,
Else for Love, and those still loved;
And those who've become King.

Death; my Death, shade of my soul.
Hold'st me in Thine arms.
Lest I take up mine 'gainst You,
My Love; my Love, stay calm;

For He hath joined the dance today,
Dancing on His own.
Death and Love show pity as
They waltz around His throne.

Love has no love for He, the King,
After how He treated Her,
And Death too has a vivid hate
From when they would confer.

Yet He, the King, steals glances at
The chair on which He sat;
And Thou, Death, glow'rest at the King
And at His feet, Thou spat'st.

The mirrors on the walls reflect
The madness ly'ng within.
But who is mad? O! Who is mad
When they are all akin?

Surprised (no, shocked!) to see them dance,
After all they (not thee) ne'er cared
For dancing, nor for romance;
It's what He's always feared.

You claim, You claim, it's not much more,
That You, Love, You love Me.
Throughout the dance, I stand alone,
Watching, being free.

When they all leave, the mirrors show
Not Death, nor Love, nor King,
But myself joined by no other
Than She who dar'st to sing.

She sits down in the broken chair
That once belonged to Him,
And now it's neither His, nor Yours;
She tempt'st me to the brim.

Death; my one, my lovely Death,
I have not known Thy solemn sting,
Else for Love, and those still loved;
And He who became King.

You and I, still You and I,
While Death stands from afar.
You and I, still You and I
Attempt to heal the scar.

Chris McMenamin

strange beings on their dreams

Strange wistful dancers weaving their dreams

Pretending that movement goes up

Diminutive,

Wishful,

Dancers making worlds

Worlds in their heads

Careful, but fierce

Hopeful, but cautious

They are the poets of the earth

Such they taste like the heavens

Oh these wistful dancers are delicious

They are food for the hungry soul

Filling it to the brim with their being

It

Is

Addictive

-J.P. Dumas

an empty ring

ours is a diamond-grafted
world
clutching so desperately to the impreg
nable
ensuring that we never lose
our jewels
and yet
we forget
we came from the biggest
change

Chris McMenamin

Sonnet XXVI: When I Should Loſe My Lady-Love

When I ſhould loſe my lady-love, eloquence her name be,
I find the hues of nature fad'th, and ſun becometh dun;
The ſky doth turn a ceaſeleß grey and darken'd clouds do come.
This thus continues on and on 'til my true love I ſee.
But often 'tis her preſence that provoketh ſuch a loß,
And often is her beauty why I have ſuch loß for words.
'Tis not for me to blame her when my praiſes can't be heard,
Nor when the verſe, now left unſaid, returns to heaven, 'loft.
And yet my love for my true love ſurpaßeth eloquence,
For but her ſmile bringeth 'bout the ſhimmer of the ſky.
O! ſuch a ſmile, I beſeech, ſhall be mine by and by.
My ſole true love, O! I declare, hath grace and gentleneß.
Prithee, my love, take 'way my words, for I need them not ſo:
Some acts of love are better ſaid while ſome are better ſhown!

Chris McMenamin

Little Lioness

She came into my life like a waking dream. It was the way the sun
played through her golden hair, as if Apollo himself had peered
down to get a glimpse of true Beauty.
She walked over and asked me why I was here…
I gazed into eyes so blue they could be a piece of the sky, I stut—tered
and said, I don't know I think I miss the people.
She smiled and skipped off. I found her fluttering nature so very enticing.

Time danced on…

The flashing lights were brighter than the starry night around us, we were
drunk, I never felt so close to heaven, as if a simple touch would be all it
took to make the universe right.
Her voice trembled as she poured her heart out to me. As she told me how
her heart wept. I couldn't understand how anyone could be foolish
enough to push her aside, because despite the sadness in her eyes
there was a light far brighter than those surrounding us burning in her soul.
I see that the heart of a lioness beats within her chest, so beautiful and
dangerous all at once...

Yet time danced on…

The lioness fading away as most beautiful memories do.

-J.P. Dumas

Sonnet VIII: My Sweet Heart's Fare

Her eyes are ſealed with nylon thread.
She ſewed them up herſelf.
Her mind is filled w'exiſtential dread:
The high point of her wealth.
She know'th that ſhe doth not love me,
Yet turn'th the other cheek.
The effort ſhe entails
Will leave me feeling weak.
Her eyes have forced the threads to break
But her lips ſtay ever ſhut.
Her gentle hands e'er harſher
Than the wriſts ſhe uſed to cut.
Her lips tell me to ſtay
While her eyes ſend me away.

Chris McMenamin

Blue dancer

ßilly ßnake with its blue eyes

ßighs, Twirling about
ßpinning like a Top

ßcreaming nothing
ßo I can help it
ßell it to all those eyes

ßtaring, Intent on making the ßnake their pet

ßome think that it will bite them
But ßilly ßnakes don't bite, they dance

ßalvation is impossible
ßo they just dance

ßpectacular
ßilly
ßad

-J.P. Dumas

Sonnet XXVIII: O! Lover Mine, O! Darling Time

Lover mine, O! darling Time, why doth thou forſake me ſo?
Although my love is ever rare,
And though oft ſaid, beyond compare,
Why doſt thou forbid me let ſee my love, prithee let know?
O! Soften'd Time, yea, conſtant Time, thy progreßion is marr'd,
For e'en as ſteady as thou tick,
The meeting and the loving mix'd.
So ſpeed ſelf up, my gracious Time, or let my love retard.
Ay, ſweetened Time, I often ſit and to your face I gaze,
O! Time, I appeal, plea, and woo
Until love be, leſt be thy doo;
Know I, 'tis thine, not Cupid's hand, who doth his lovers ſave.
Then beg thee now, O! gentle Time,
Liſten to reaſon, and to rhyme.

Chris McMenamin

Beautiful Creatures

If there is one thing I have learned in my twin-
decades it is that the world
is filled with big faraway places
I refer not to countries or continents; instead the
faraway places I of which I dream are the ones
found in each other's eyes
In the wild souls of beautiful creatures
I have met many such beings; all of them
opened my eyes to galaxies of hidden wonders
Like the beautiful creatures they are however
they often disappear into the night
ripping away the worlds I found within them
Left with only the fading memories of flowers
and the dreams of a lioness' roar
Such is the tragedy of exploring faraway places
I suppose, no matter how wonderfully breath
taking a place is eventually you have to return
home
Each of these journeys preparing us for the next,
until one day we find a faraway place we simply

refuse to

leave

-J.P. Dumas

집

엄마 집

아빠 집

아이 집?

어디가 아이 집?

가 가 가

SW

The Labyrinth II: This gift, unto sphere, I endow

I

This gift, unto sphere, I endow; a sphere unlike the heaven's heirs:
She sits in centre of the world and takes one's pain and worldly fears.
Yet she imparts no knowledge, nay, she speaks nothing at all.
Wond'rous sphere! Yea, wise old sphere! I turn 'way from the wall.

II

In comfort, now that fears are safe; from whom, I daren't ask,
I leave the sphere to suffer, 'lone, and well, she knows the task.
But these fears have import to me, and I leave with remorse,
Yet I know they have weighed me down. I turn to face my course.

Chris McMenamin

I'm glad I met you

I didn't say - I loved you

But I hoped you knew

-

MH

Sonnet XXVII: I need not have these words

I need not have these words to woo a woman lest she be
A lover unalike the likes of those I've loved afore.
Alas, my love is so much more, and so these words I need
If I have want for my dear love to ever me adore.
My love, e'er sweet, I long to meet when I am free and 'lone,
Or when the day (quite soon, I pray) comes to make real my dreams.
Such dreams in which my love is played and viv'dly to her shown,
as games with joy, yet rancor made, disported to extremes.
Thus, love, I woo, and picture you with skin as fair as wings
From swans who tread the waters, O!, so lightly as angels
Who glow so bright, as though your eyes; play holy songs and sing
Almost as with the sweetness that your lips and voice involve.
Why, I do need these words to woo my untellable love.
O! Thus it still always has been, and will, always, be thus.

Chris McMenamin

A Dialogue Between a Cursèd Man and His Shade

CHORUS
A cursèd man once walked along
To try and right all of his wrongs.
He turned around to glance behind:
His enemy sprang from his mind.

CURSÈD MAN
What are you doing here, today?
I do not want to see your face.
I bid you leave, you go away
For I no longer have my grace.

HIS SHADE
I am your soul, your shade, your mind.
I am your death; you keep me kind.
I am he who you try to find.
I am you, our selves intertwined.

CURSÈD MAN
And if you were to die a death:
A knife into your back or side;
For this to be your final breath,
Would you deride, or death decide?

HIS SHADE
Your blade would pierce not skin, nor bone;
Your blade would pierce my love alone.

CURSÈD MAN
Are you really whom I disdain?
Perhaps a lesson from my pain?

HIS SHADE
I am not whom you think I am,
I know not how I look to you,
But know it is who you condemn,
Who you struggle to love anew.

CURSÈD MAN
But why would you take such a form?
So as to cause me more distress?
Tell me now! I bid you inform
Why I must take this final test.

HIS SHADE
Because you cannot love yourself.
Because you must love me foremost.

I like it when, in your shade, I dwell
You make the kindest of all hosts.

When I am cast by you, I feel
You lead me safe from harm, to heal.

CHORUS
The shadow took a step too far,
He found the man, and chose to mar.
The shadow took a step too far,
Marked by the shadow, shadow's scar.

Memories of falling in love: Part five

"End."

There is a difference between falling in love and loving someone. Falling in love is a rush of new experiences fuelled by wild emotion. Time erodes at this wild emotion and refines it into love. Love is more than just wild passion or a string of three words we say to get our way, it is a bond where mind and soul become indistinguishable. This bond makes you feel safe, comfortable and it can overcome any obstacle. When this bond is severed however it leaves a mark on your very soul.

We became lost in our togetherness, weeks turned to months and I'd long to spend every second with you. We danced, we sang, we made love and we grew closer than I ever imagined possible. My heart was no longer flustered when I saw you, instead it filled up with warmth as if I had arrived home. With comfort however comes challenge and we fought as much as we loved. Often the arguments were pointless, about pointless things. Oh, but how they stirred the raw, wild emotions we once felt. We were standing in the same spot where we first kissed when it happened. "We need to break up." Five words that no one could have prepared me for. Five words that shattered my heart. Five words that to this day have claimed a part of me...

-J.P. Dumas

To Dream

I realised that to dream about you was to dream about
everything beautiful and to find amongst all these beautiful
things, you were fairer still.

so extraordinary in that moment that to dream about
you, was like staring into the eyes of a god and realizing that you
and she were one and the same.

I stood there in that fleeting moment of perfection with eyes met
and hearts intertwined, wanting only to speak these words.
Yet I pulled away because I knew dreaming about you would be

the end of me.

-J.P. Dumas

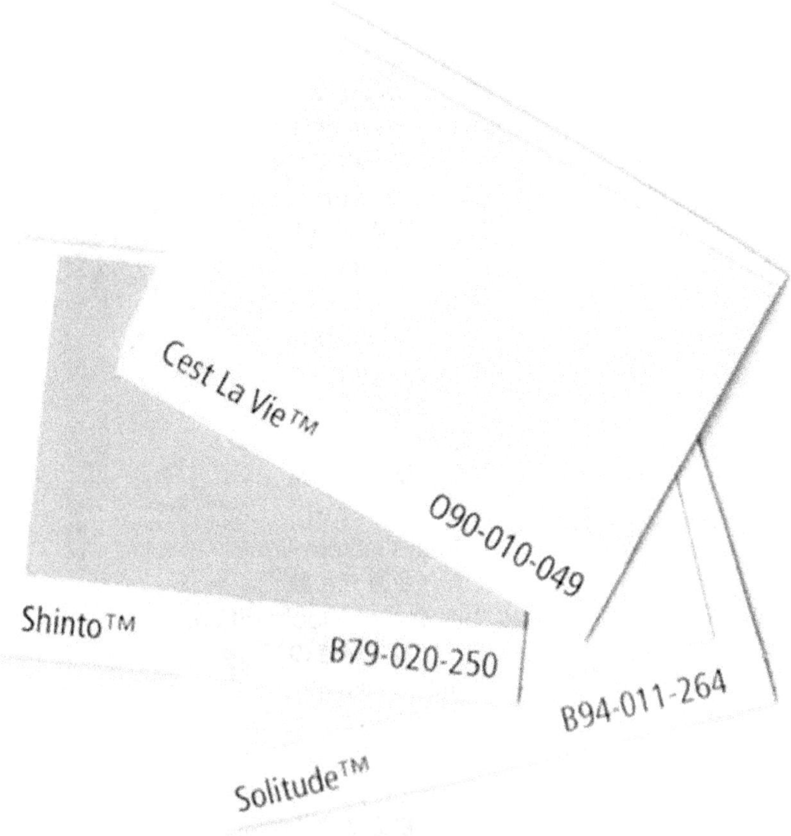
Cest La Vie™
090-010-049
Shinto™
B79-020-250
B94-011-264
Solitude™

Seasonal Rebirth

Seasonal rebirth
季節の復活
Allows opportunity
新たなスタート
To start something new
収容します
☼
Blossom haze flowers
花曇り住む
Inside oneself as tea leaves
ないぶのなかで
Are plucked from bushes
間中茶つみ
☼
A fragrant breeze shifts
薫風のせい
The fifth-month darkness to one
五月闇うごかす
And to one's new tea
誰に又新茶
☼
In this lantern-light
名月です妙
The harvest moon looks different
灯篭の輝きの下
Still one cuts the rice
刈米つづく
☼
First snow withers fields
初雪は作る
Early plum blossoms flourish
彼の又そうばい
Out of fallen leaves
孰隠し落葉

Chris McMenamin

Il sogno

Reality became us,
that old place in my heart stirs again.
Still empty after all this time.
Part of me still belongs only to you.

Hopelessness lashing out at hearts

I used to blame you for that; I was merely the beast that you created…
Scorned by love so I scorned it.

Yet after all this time I still smile when I think of our afternoons in bed,
as the long bus rides in-between our homes
draw me into a dream.
Il sogno.

-J.P. Dumas

lágrimas de azúcar (sugar tears)

¿Lloras, Lolita? wet dish rag sighs, Lolita
the empty dishes speak

no, no, mi niño, the sun was in my eyes –
sunbeam hits the sugarpane glass of the –
light up the dust – of the windowsill,
good enough to lick

lloras, Lolita, tú de los suspiros
tú del agua, dámelo
las mujeres son sombras,
¿Por qué quieres agua?

To drink, only a little, a little now to drink.

Don't cry, Lolita
You'll rise, Lolita
One day one sugarbeam morning
Don't cry, Lolita,
You're alive, Lolita

(No llores, Lolita,
O te golpeo, Lolita)

Shh, shh, niño, shhh now, daddy's coming

Not without lemon, take the tea wet armpits
dishrag in the sink
autumn leaves pull the sugar window closer.

Lolita, Lolita, sighs in the night, Lolita
dulce el dolor, stiffening plaster tears
Stay strong babe, hold the window frame –
Don't let him see your pain –

Why are you crying, Lolita?
Why are you crying, Mama, why?

¡Sí, lloro! Sí lloro! Si ella llora!
¡Sí!

I'm not crying, my Darling
Look, it's the raindrops on the sugar glass
Making the teardrops run

SW

In The End/What's Yours Is Mine

The beginning was my mothers and
I was a bird flown straight out of heaven
Through distilled rainwater I
Was the air through a sea shell and
I is serene

The middle was all mine a running book
Running races and through gravel cutting I
I drip home

I was a running tap
And a crumbling family
I was pretty debris on your pretty hips

Distilled fire city begins
Simmering cowardly and I
Cutting secrets slipping

An I awaits yours crumbling bird
An I will make your coffee sweeter

Now
A better I is coming
I am not pretty debris I is peeling
Peeling through the air I is not the one I knew
I is not the I you knew
Before I
I is a bird flown
Is a bird flown through fire I
I is my mother and I is all mine
And I am here.

The beginning was my mothers,
The other bits were just about mine,
But the end, that was yours -
And I am a bird flown straight out of heaven
So thank you.

The Veritable Truth Of Living

begin in the – cup of tea – pleasure - morning – tips – on there

crushed tapestries of sky - blue rocket – bear it up –

water – globe exists - tea water – in the darkness –

people and stars matter

- begin.

begin – in the cup of tea - morning – drink it up, press it

to the blossoming ceiling

hope

atlas

bears the weight.

SW

A Mother's Song: Lorca's "Romance de la Luna, Luna"

Shh child shh shut your eyes
Close your ears to the drum
Put away your old tin soldiers
The moon and night have come.

Pure lilies crest the open plain,
Strut their necklaces and rings
Earth dreams dreams dipped in silver –
A little lone bird sings.

Rest your head on your mother's breast
Ignore the sky, my dear
Lest the gypsies should come steal you
Their horses near, I fear!

Come away from the window, child
Lie down, your eyes shut tight
Dream of pretty trinkets
Forget the gypsy fires alight.

But now the moon moves through the white clouds
The lewd moon is coming near
Oh watch out, my little child!
The moon too wants you, I fear!

Ah, the trees all quiver
I hear the gypsies cry
The starchy stars above me
Wrench out a mother's cry.

Oh my child, must I lose you!
Must you go away?
Take pity on your mother's tears
Her hair all turning grey!

Hard the white moon hard
Child, why do you stand?
The gypsies' cries fade far away
And, the moon, she takes your hand.

SW

À Travers les Détours de l'Art

« La vie d'un homme est seulement
une marche lente à redécouvrir,
à travers les détours de l'art,
ces deux ou trois images merveilleuses et simples
en présence de lesquelles son cœur d'abord ouvert. »
— Camus

Les parfums étoffé et somptueux
de café noir du piston
a pris au piège tout ton être.
Tu n'as jamais aimé le café.
Tu as fermé les yeux
et senti ton rythme cardiaque ralenti.
Tes orteils fléchis et la tête inclinée vers l'arrière.
Tu ouvris les yeux
à une pièce familière
et un visage connu.
Ce fut la première image.
Non, la première scène :
l'odeur du café et la vue de son visage
qui était caressé par les rayons du soleil
qui se sont échappés entre les rideaux.
Le sens du soleil filtré sur ton visage
et le bruit sourd du monde extérieur
étant occupé et chaotique
tout en que vous étiez assis en silence.

Dans la deuxième scène,
ce baiser
était considérablement comme beaucoup d'autres
que vous avez partagé,
mais pendant ce baiser
tu réalisé la profondeur
à travers lequel
tu l'avais aimé.
Toutes les sensations corporelles tu as vécu.
Le noir à l'intérieur de tes paupières.
Son parfum qui émanait
de son cou à tes narines.
Sa bouche douce et chaude,
ce qui correspond avec tes lèvres gercées.
Ses cheveux
qui chatouillaient
contre ton cou.
Ses doigts qui retracées ton peau.
Cette agglomération
simultanée des sentiments séparés,
et chaque a été accentué
comme si les rideaux avaient été ouvertes
et la chambre
était baignée de lumière lorsque,
en réalité,
les lumières étaient éteintes et le monde était silencieux.

Un jour
ensoleillé sur la place d'une gare en plein air.
Une image
que tu associes avec aucun autre sens.
Une salle
de spectacle agréable qui est associé
à une mémoire bien trop déplaisante.
Mais une image toutefois.
La résiliation de ta vie.
Et donc on écrit.
Tu écris redécouvrir l'amour même si tu dois vivre à
travers le déchirement.

Chris McMenamin

THE POEM OF THE FUTURE

BEGINS in dustbins, in ashes
seized anew from liquidating sunsets
snatch the rosebud blush, trap it in
a jar, put it away, for future purposes.

IN THE FUTURE

PAINT ashes over skin
paint face, cheeks, mouth, neck, chest –
black, but let the
white ribs poke through –
draw them from out, carefully,
bone flowers like flesh.

sunset rises, up from bellies of feet,
to waist, to arms, to neck,
feed the cacophony of colour.

from the ashes – cherry blossoms
from the ashes – raging rampant red camellias
and yellow sunflowers.

TAKE the glow of the sunset
mix colours on skin
pour it over hair –
the poem walks, talks
the poem is a sun goddess
hair black, hair split with flowers
the goddess shouts, cries
breathes fog against the jar
crack it wide **OPEN**

SW

Poem for the Night

Alles is goed, kind.
Slaap met een rustige hart
en 'n stil gees.

Alles is kalm, lief kind.
De wilde dieren zijn onderwonnen
en nou moet jy slaap.

Alles is nog steeds, kind.
Slaap, anders worden genomen
door mythische wezens.

Alle rustige, lief kind.
Jou huil het opgehou
en jy het jou bed verlaat.

Chris McMenamin

she grows

blossoming sprout, you surpass me
still a little bumpy, edges still a little coarse
still barefoot shell crushed but eyelashes brush the stars

you need someone to teach you make up tricks
    not me
    too late for me but you you have
unwritten pathways to discover

smaller echo of my shape, bent out, rearranged
i will walk the long roads with you
but i cannot follow you into the sky

SW

You / twisting turning yellow honey coloured hair

the sky wakes up blushing You

unfold life like newspaper

You a ball of string You a picture someone draw on You
the binding holding the world together You the glue You
the silk of hair You can't stop minding winding around fingers,
keep twirling don't break the chain – You
You the brown tide mark of the yellow honey dye shy of the crown
roll a die roll a die
only covers half of You.

You a moving somewhere
not sure
where

You a blue map of veins across shoulders collarbone breaks
back into the tops of arms veins reaching intertwining
He stretch You back to see the whiteness the bareness, say look, look, He see
the curve the shape You
You see the veins holding You together –
a lily You unread atlas with dustjacket on You –

You a bookshelf with the books all covered spines facing back You
a mystery You is not what You think You know.

You is the way the rusted brass of your hair flashes white gold

You the gold –

You is the song outside the door the light
under the gap but You is not brave enough to grab it You
still afraid   You still scared by the ring of shadow.

Your hair Your hair Your hair
You is Your hair.

twisting twisting twisting – still look smooth. Still Growing, Growing
hair don't know
                    where it's going

SW

Lullaby

Melava inan enansal
ir su araval tu elvaral
by lies Vereevig
Eg songane søkte
Te sing fir die gode
Vi dýr ennui nu Anor

Alt veit eg,
Mala taren aravas,
So kom, sit by my.
Laat my synge fir jou!
in doot slaap slynge my
waar ma ghilas, da'len

Ma garas mir renan
my naam fir jou vhenas,
Athan eryd berge staap,
Ara ma'athlan tuis,
Når du ved Helgrindi star,
Sal ek you huistoe roep

emma ir abelas
Cormamin niuve tenna' ta elea lle au'
Quel kaima

-J.P. Dumas

do you need me to stay?

do you need me to stay by your side?
protect you from things
in your wardrobe, or under your bed?
do you need me to stay by your side?
to thrust you aside
at the sight of the oncoming train?
to jump into the path
of the rocks and the stones?
do you need me to stay by your side?
to save you from evil?

do you need me to hide from your sight?
allow you to face this world on your own?
do you need me to hide from your sight?
to remain at a distance
while you dodge the train?
to hold back tears
as you try catching the stones?
do you need me at all?

Chris McMenamin

D C

O R

N A

O C

T K

tea cup hold my balance in

fine tight rope like fine china

i did eat too many biscuits

tea helps me forget is

superglue my heart

cup me keep the boiling inside let the

steam refresh me not break

SW

The key, the key! — Chris M.

Il y a un pouvoir dans ces mots

of the frustum. Looking at the same part of the formula, we may be moved to write it also in the form

$$\pi(R + r) = 2\pi \frac{R + r}{2}$$

that is the *perimeter of the mid-section* of the frustum. (We call here mid-section the intersection of the frustum with a plane which is parallel both to the lower base and to the upper base of the frustum and bisects the altitude.)

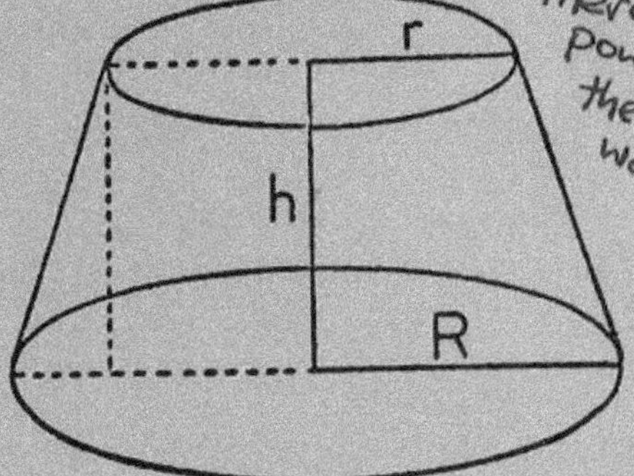

There is a power in these words and I have lost the key

FIG. 12

et j'ai perdu

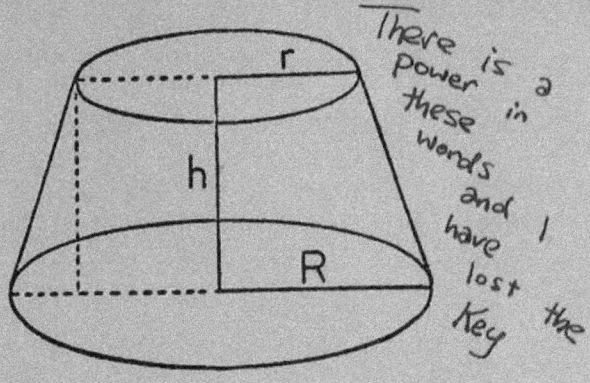

Having found new interpretations of various parts, we may see now the whole formula in a different light. We may read it thus:

Area = Perimeter of mid-section × Slant height.

We may recall here the rule for the trapezoid:

Area = Middle-line × Altitude.

la clé

(The middle-line is parallel to the two parallel sides of the trapezoid and bisects the altitude.) Seeing intuitively the analogy of both statements, that about the frustum and that about the trapezoid, we see the whole result about the frustum "almost at a glance." That is, we feel

BICYCLES IN SHANGHAI

Simple dream pain
Can you imagine
The forgetting, or the numbness of your legs

The smog is potent this time of year
It's presence
That cool 30 degrees

A video
Of the accident
Nobody dares look

Grey pain
Black and white pain
Watch dry the paint

Shaky hands the both now
Bacon and eggs a Western delight
Some untranslated communication

These eggs you know
Don't spoil the bacon
We've had enough rice this week

Picture a room with
POLICE INTERROGATOR
And the translator

Is it darkened
Spotlight centred
Something to fear

Something as like a dream
What do you remember
What did you film

Tell them of the news
No Google or Facebook
These are not China's friends

蛋 / dàn
Once more
Still a refresher

The police lawyers return
Lasers for fingertips
They don't understand

How many bicycles in Shanghai
A score of millions of people
And these two that I love

How can you imagine
The forgetting
Or the numbness of your legs

七月二十一日上海 / Qī yuè èrshíyī rì shànghǎi
出租车相撞交通事故 / Chūzū chē xiāng zhuàng jiāotōng shìgù
事故现场 / Shìgù xiànchǎng

Two taxis
In separate rooms
Then the ICU

Floor two
Floor seven
They saw each other once

Chris McMenamin

Memories

Time erodes at this wild emotion,
nothing more than a biological Inevitability
There is rain, when falling in love.
Though that doesn't matter,
Through giggles and smiles we were dancing in the rain.
The storm fuelled our bond.
Our two orbits so close,
that the universe would envy us
My bedroom the seat of divinity

Time may erode our love
It may burn the home I found in you
It may scatter our footsteps from the sand
But it cannot erase us of our shared divinity
Memories of your soul will forever kindle that fire.

-J.P. Dumas

Farewell

Soos ons hier sit by die fuur
En droom oor die verlede
Our hearts heavy with joy and sorrow in equal parts
For a new adventure en die lewe wat on los.

Tell me, van die blou lig en die wolke
Vertel my, about the blue ocean and the waves
Laat my leer.
Laat my weet.
Because the time spent here is irreplaceable
But our time,
Ons tuid,
Is over.

So I raise my cup in hand, een laaste keer.
En sit for a moment longer.
Hoop, hoping that the memories of this place
Nooit weg raak nie,
From the smiles to the tears
this is home.
Hier in n fer weg land…

-J.P. Dumas

the girl

she is alive hair catching wind
only exists to be like this only exists summer
like a song invincible unconquerable
like breath like
sunlight
is
so
much
more alive
life swells in her
breast pick a flower
grown in cracks
spilling over
skirts
perched on window
ledges sinew and flesh that
thrum and violets roses lilies and
daffodils flowers bloom on her skin are
woven in her skirt blows in the wind like
a song there in the woods in the leaves
a song that goes on forever who has she
to fear because she is ALIVE ALIVE ALIVE

l e w
t o
s r
u s d
r
w i d
e n
h
t g
i n l l r
t l o w
h w
e y

g g g g g g g g g g g
r r r r r r r r r r r r r r r r r r r r r
a a a a a a a a a a a a a a a a a a a a a
s s s s s s s s s s s s s s s s s s s s s
s s s s s s s s s s s

and death

t a

r l

o but behind her

m lurks death with skull

m and hollow eyes

s a i hollow cheeks he

d r e follows the

r girl

o

w he follows her across mountains and valleys

fingers always reaching out

always one step to

closer closer touch

time ticks her

and

o t death

h not

e r reach ing

t quite but

h i he will

n just give

g him time

s death has

d a hollow

i e heart

g g g g g g g g g g g

r r r r r r r r r r r r r r r r r r r

a a a a a a a a a a a a a a a a a a a a

s s s s s s s s s s s s s s s s s s s s s

s s s s s s s s s s s

-SW

Liefde

drie hours
buried beneath its sheets.
who can face time and erase its marks?
who can face time and erase its eyes?
the eyes that held me Down on the floor

eienaar is what it's called.
it calls me nothing.
crawl, nothing, make it worth it!
crawl, niks kind, it enjoys the way you cry!
yoU belong beneath this torment!
i don't want to be near it
i did nothing, i deserve to leave it.

honey, kom trug na my hart toe!
yesterday, i ran through the forest and played my ballads to the eager wesens
i touch the roots of their oak, roots of the oak don't touch back
spinning, spinning. the tree admires.
It watches on devious
waiting for me, wolf

the thing, Vol fet slang sheltering me waiting for its appetite
it made me feel feilig like it wouldn't hurt me
it swept me up and kept me from harm's way in the forest of the nasty wesens
i should be grateful.

It says it loves me very much
that my nothingness makes me perfect for it
if i give you what you know you want wilL you cry
niks kind will you stay with me?

to say the name of evil
DUIVIL

-J.P. Dumas

there are so many poems about fish

I do not feel like I am——
writing——I am
writing New Zealand Poetry——I am
a New Zealand Poet——I do not feel
like——I——am

writing poetry————when I read this,
I hear
the——Tusiatas——and Tusitalas——
of my world————I do not hear
my——
my——
poetry.

Chris McMenamin

just this

now
it is the quiet time of the evening.

now
everyone is finishing their dinner
and you stand on the shore before the sea
throwing pebbles in the waves,
marvelling at the fresh smell and yet –
the closeness of the sunset.

it is almost
dark,
the light beams that pushed whole and perfect
against the incoming tide of night
are dying.
the seaweed on the shore
clumps in dark pools, resigned,
surrendered to the wanting of the current –
rise and crash
and rise again.
the mounds of sand shaped by little hands
melt like crushed obsidian.
shells, trees, people, waves,
all are coolly tucked away, under the blanket
of the oncoming dusk.

as you watch
the waves give up the shore, shrug off the sun's beams
you reach out your palm to catch them, return
empty.

as you watch
the sun abandons the beach
to the night

SW

Shadow

Lonely old shadow

Dipping fingers in the cherry blossoms' bleached redness

Day lengthens, grow older, shadow

Lost in darkness

Still alone.

SW

the red and white and yellow poppies on my desk in a vase that is tied with an orange ribbon

the poppies

are nice.

SW

A Dialogue Between Mine Eye and Inner Truth

CHORUS
The earth and heav'n are set apart as dru'd, to angel, frays.
The two from diff'rent substance make, desir' take, promise say.
The angel's name is Inner Truth, the druid is Mine Eye.
This dialogue shall end in death, for one shall choose to die.

MINE EYE
I prithee answer, Inner Truth, why my life, thou abhor,
And fill with such sweet emptiness as thus which thou display.
Such emptiness I've learned to love, yet hold the want to slay,
So as to find true happiness, and my old self, restore.
I prithee answer, Inner Truth, and give thy reason why
Such pain has fallen down on me, from heaven e'er above.

INNER TRUTH
The answer, dear, is found within the swelling of my love;
Not even I could dare decry the valour of Mine Eye,
So know that it was not my hand that caused such emptiness.

MINE EYE
On whom, then, may I lay the blame for causing my distress?

CHORUS
The druid laments to the sky, from his dead, desert plain.
The dry, cracked earth on which he walks will be his barren bane.
He looks upon the cloudless sky, and to the heavens there:
Radiant beams and trumpet swells abolish any fear.

INNER TRUTH
My love for thee can prove that thy state is not heaven sent;
O! such an act, to angels, is a move we could not deign,
Alas I can but ponder who could realise thy pain.
O! Sole this man, or woman so, could e'er, said pain, relent.

CHORUS
Now fallen to the crackèd floor, the druid in his might,
To realise it was hisself who hindered his own sight.
With draining hope left to pursue the life he could have owned,
He lies alone in 'ttempt to find a comfort in his bones.

MINE EYE
The choice that I now face is neither noble, nor is brave,
Yet this mistake that I have made will haunt me to my grave.

CHORUS
O! Inner Truth's soft, feathered wings now shelter from the sun.
The angel falls of own accord, and therefore is made one
With druid lying still with no hope to remain alive.
O! Inner Truth, did Eye revive, yet did himself, of life, deprive.

Chris McMenamin

SEASON NOTEBOOK

Autumn

the roses

in the vase on the windowsill are cupped

in the mist and in the stone

a lantern shines.

pour the roses into wine glasses

seize the stems, the leafy twists are drunk by the sound

of your

voice

Winter

the windowpane shudders

under the weight of raindrops glassy and

shivering like opals

and the aching clouds wring their hands and demand attention.

walk north wearing bare feet, drink the wine

clamber

white bedclothes, stained by

scarlet sips.

here is the wood, impregnable.

split it into pieces

feed the crimson flames.

Spring, almost Summer

like spring showers, like summer rain

wash the bedsheets

stop up the lid of the dripping sky

unleash the vine, plant the roses

on a sparkling bed of white.

let me in.

when summer comes

let me in.

SW

Wet N Wild™ B49-089-260

Eastern Blue™ B59-088-212

Decadence™ B37-091-284

This Is Where We Come From

When he says he is from "Whack-a-tain" I can feel my great grandmother's anger broiling in my gut.
He says he "has always pronounced it like that"
As if what is right, is simply what we have always done -
Since before our nuclear families shamed you for your fluidity, before we emasculated your sacred carvings, and infiltrated your spirituality with our own, before our smacking parents, and our strange labels arrived on the shores of Gisborne and latched onto things they did not understand
Things have not always been like this
And I can feel the anger of her people – our people – inside of me.

You, Koro, are from *Whakatane*
Born between Earth Mother and Sky Father
Ranginui and Papatuanuku shaped each of your mother's brave thighs
Her bridgeless nose
Her strong frame
And I can feel the anger of your people inside of me, Tūmatauenga
As you too will to destroy those who bore you.

When I visit the Marae on a Thursday, he asks for us to introduce ourselves with our sacred body of water - our sacred mountain
I cannot remember my mihi anymore.

We have twinked over a war won by criminals
And poured bleach down the throat of a culture that was too colourful for us to understand
But our agreement is in writing on crisp white parchment –
And we are not ashamed enough to change *what it is that we have always done.*

We are the visitors here
The people welcome us but we do not turn up to be welcomed
The 9AM powhiri is empty of Pakeha
and we forget to take off our Chuck Taylors as we step into the Wharenui on a Thursday afternoon.

Ko Maungawhau te māunga
Ko Waikato te awa
Ko Waikato tōku iwi

Nō Tamaki-makau-rau ahau
Ko Molly tōku ingoa

Mō taku hē, mō taku hē

- MH

Strange shadow

Treats are everywhere
How am I supposed to stop indulging?

A bite here,
a nibble there.
Sweet delectable,
Mouth-watering treats!

I don't think anyone understands
I won't stop
Until the treats
Are all
Gone.

-J.P. Dumas

Sonnet XX: Dawn

What they told us not was that
Stars are embraces we've never had.
Think thy brightest memories,
These are stars thou scarcely see.
Think the loves that thou have felt,
Now dimmer than Orion's Belt.
Pray view the stars, shining strong:
The love for which you dearly long.
Bathing in crepuscular light:
Waiting, waiting for the night.
Soft sand lies beneath thy feet;
Waiting for new stars to meet.
Greet thy love and ocean waves:
Paradise: true Love's true race.

Chris McMenamin

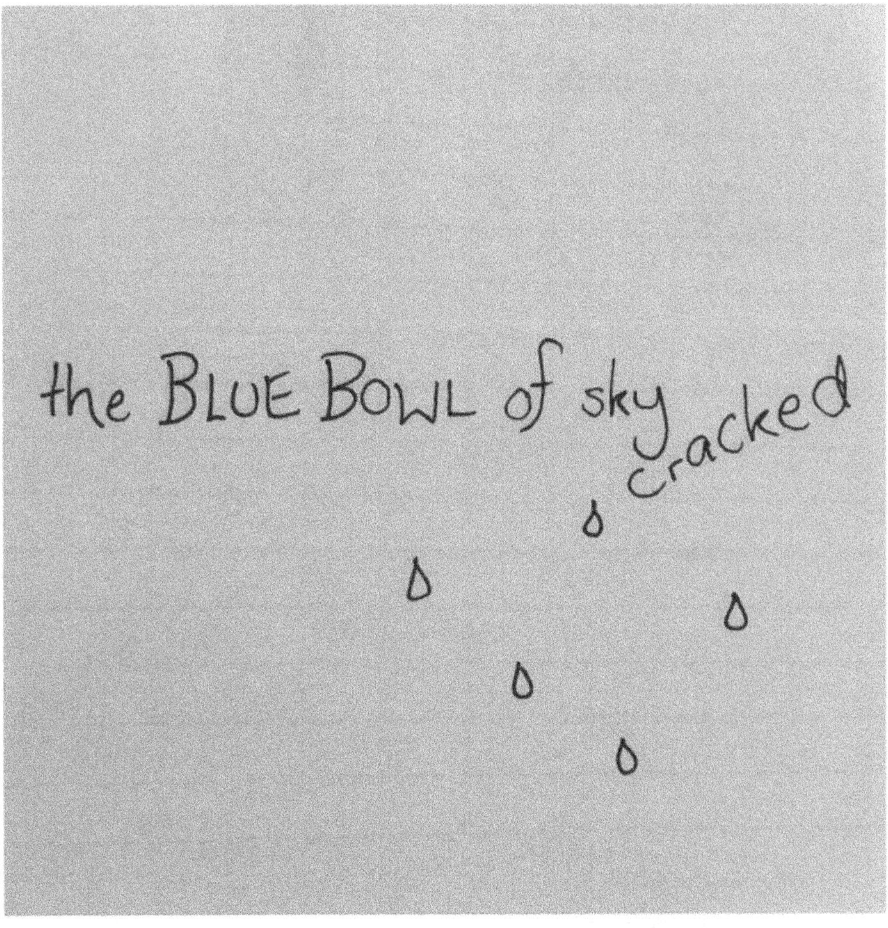
the BLUE BOWL of sky
cracked

SW

This Cup

I

*

in the brokenness of this cup
we find flaws in ourself
kintsugi

*

i think of rowan williams
of webs of intentions
and that i am my past

*

in this cup we hold
warm with mulled wine
a lightness of head

*

in the shape of my hands
a cup that is full will overflow
open shaky hands wide

*

magnetic pulling
these hand-cups will not let go
of imbedded actions

*

let go, let go
a cup that is full will surely overflow
raise my hands by my head

*

now our mind is clear
now our being can be free
of biting reactions

*

you both sit
she pours her cup in yours
you pour half back

*

*

the bitter cup
requires more vinegar
to resemble gethsemane

*

i am joyed with the now
my cup doth overflow with blessings
it pours over the stones

*

i hold a cup on Michaelmas
and pray for him
and hold an empty stein

*

i want to kiss the glass
instead i hold it to my nose
we share one breath

*

i thank and love
and ask that i can love
and that Love will protect him

*

i hold an empty teacup
and give thanks
and remember

*

i hold my hands out
but cannot receive
they have filled again

*

we empty the patterns
and ask to not gnash back
to be filled anew

*

Chris McMenamin

This Cup

II

*

therefore we find
beauty in the brokenness
of our own self

*

and in the newness
of life as gold-plated betters-than
the past is a web

*

holding a glass of port
feels different still
cool in our hand

*

sip the sweet wines
the mulled and the port
remember that bitter cup

*

an overlapping of the hands
now a different vessel
they move aside

*

i
did not kiss
the stein

*

this cup holds
earl grey with rose and cornflower
shared with friends

*

that cup holds
jasm-oolong with rose as well
my personal blend

*

i jokingly say
goodbye, goodbye
to the past therefore myself

*

singing bowls
and crystal bowls
and glass harps

*

fountain trickle
and something that once
resembled a melody

*

light is let in
through our cracks
through our flaws

*

friends love the light
the hope
the beauty in scars

*

she raises to your lip
paper cup
you drink thirstily

*

the stones are wet
the vase is fuller even now
flood into silver bowl below

*

the Table remains
uneaten-from
the communion is not assembled

*

Chris McMenamin

This Cup

III

*

some of us are shattered
not beyond repair
when in solace

*

she extends her hands
and receives that cup you filled
press paper to lips

*

this gathering
repairs us
who wish reparation

*

the stein remains empty
not untouched
but empty

*

we are listening now
to this cup, this cup
i wanna drink it up

*

the water in the stone-vase
is filled to the brim
and the silver underneath

*

the Table hath been touched
but not eaten
and hath touched

*

the bitter cup
lacks vinegar still
but brings pain

*

*

remind us cup
to hold our pain in our mouths
and live

*

the teacup rests on saucer
clinking has ceased
this cup, this cup

*

kintsugi lines remind us to find
in our cracks
beauty

*

the giving and receiving
and the port
holding glass

*

two-hand glass guzzled
i hold its fruit
i taste it

*

the hands
becoming this cup
letting go

*

no more can go in
our hand falls slowly
then the other hand

*

all the while a master potter
creates distorted bowls
on floating muslin

*

Chris McMenamin

Sea-worn stones

Like wise men's eyes
You sit, in hand.

Perfumed with the sea, silt,
Years of ocean waves rubbed in.
Smoothed into concave
Rocked with grit.

Soft blue pebbles,
Here you are, treasure
Made to fill pirate palms, run
With cracks, made to complete
The shallow cavern of my hand –

I bury you again
Beneath the rolling sand.

SW

A Dialogue Between True Soul and True Body

CHORUS
From blue-grassed hills, I do observe
The blood-soaked, blood-stained battleground.
True Body dons a shield e'er round:
Red and black, with golden curve.
A sword is claimed by Soul e'er True,
Wrought from steel, and jew'l encrusted:
Heaven's sword, by Michael, lusted.
Prepare thyselves, war starts anew.

SOUL
I should like to live a life
As pure as any soul can live.
But this, dear Body, thou forbid;
'tis thou, not I, wh'invoked this strife.

BODY
What do I restrict from you?
I have my needs and fill them so.

SOUL
As when the lion hunts? Lo!
Men of wits, many lions, slew.
Compare thyself not to a gracious beast,
Th'art no more than a woeful worm,
At whose sight, my stomach turns.
Disdain, the most. Hatred, the least.

BODY
If lions be devils, be it so, sir:
Rather a devil in your bed
Than unknown devil in your head.
Befriend the devil that you know, sir.

SOUL
I've never met such a brute
In all the time I was awake.

BODY
Best you choose, this option, take
Than let the devil, you, pollute
In vile dreams with no avail.

SOUL
And sink down to the dreamer's level?
I have no want to know the devil,
Let alone to bow, and hail.

CHORUS
Alas! True Body's injured now,
The weight of shield too hard to bear.
True Body, know thy death is near.
Soul, with death, your sword, endow.

BODY
Though it brings you such distaste,
Picture love throughout night's start.
Nights move together; days apart -
Such torment that, your days, you'd waste.
I pray, take not the final kill,
Not mere for murder's worse than death
In th'eye of Giver of Breath,
But misfortune, my blood will spill.

SOUL
Perhaps death is more apt than
The endless torment thou predict,
After all, the two conflict.

BODY
This is the better plan.

SOUL
Thus, with reluctance, I concede,
Yet only 'til the time is right.
I still shall live within the light
And fulfil all thine evil needs.

CHORUS
O! Take pity on False Soul,
For he has signed the devil's deal!
Fallen to the ground, his steel,
Which, only now, has Body stole.
The final strike upon his head.
Cry now tears of grief, my friends,
For purity has reached her end,
As Soul, now False, becomes dead.
Mourn the loss that we all face.
True Body lives his perfect day:
No Soul to stand within his way.
Mourn the loss that we all face.

Chris McMenamin

The decline of Earth

There were three hundred and fourteen

Brave
Blue
Battles

They aren't talked about much.

-J.P. Dumas

Life amongst the Waves

Will you come with me out past the
buoy, boy?

Is this the summer of you and me?

Can you find me amongst the white wash,
boy?

Or will you let me drift out to sea?

Will you dip your toe in the salt, boy?

Or is your reputation too grand?

Where is the life in the summer, boy?

If you stay warm and cool on dry land?

Sing songs like the sounds of water,
boy?

Sing songs like they're written for
me?

Do I live for the sound of your
whisper, boy?

Don't you live for the sound of the
sea?

Will this whirlpool ever unfurl, boy?

Will you apologise for what you said?

Will you drown me in the ocean, boy?

Or leave me here for dead?

Will you bury me with go-pros and
wedding rings?

Will you meet me back here by the sea?

Do you ever dream about death, boy?

Will you ever dream about me?

\- MH

Sonnet XXXVIII: O! Choleric 'A' Mutilated

In an amalgam of the poet ry of the past——a

language-mixing of   codes

not yet understood——the poem

of the
          present.

The presence of zazen in a German

surname——a listening to the people

before——an imaginingingingingingof

possibility of words   on
                                   words.

Such an advanced,   neuroscientific   understanding

of how words affect——a contr   ol

to tickle the brain in   all   the
right ways——

a heart——beat on a leash.

A remembering of——a sudden realisation——

the future.

~ 12b ~

Chris McMenamin

how heavy the water

how heavy the water is around her
is immaterial when you consider how much her heart weighs
        I'm about to fall, it says.
        I think everything hurts if you hold it tight enough, she thinks.

as a girl she believed
she heard angels in the burning shower water singing.
she thinks, standing in the shower, how
nobody crosses oceans nowadays
        he
and her in the churning sea
        drifting apart like
drops of drain water
like sand in a titanic tide
imagining her meeting him like the first notes of a song
a maiden voyage bound for unfathomable shores,
like angels' singing –

fades into the pit pat pat of droplets hitting shower cap.

when she turns off the shower
the angels disappear.

SW

IN A SHACK BY A LAKE

He could not imagine
the fish inside the shack were alive,
nor anything inside.

But he could see the fish in their
silver hats, purple boots, and tawny cats on their shoulders.
And in the distance,

he saw a woman:
thorns, or silk, or ribbons in her hair.
He could not tell.
Much of the lake was overcome.
A loss of words stopped his movement.

Perhaps there is a connection between the boots,
the cats, and the auburn shade, free to dance.

Walking past her at the far edge
was another, more afraid.

The fish, the other spoke.
There's something in the fish.

There is no time in the composition.
The composition consists only of a single harmonic explosion
away from anything you know as familiar,

towards the unknown.
Towards the fish, and the cats,
the purple boots, the silver hats.

Chris McMenamin

Memories of falling in love: Part two

"Dancing in the rain."

There is this overwhelming desire to move when you are falling in love, as if your senses become more attuned with the earth, as if everything around you is more alive.

Sitting there in a tiny little coffee shop, staring into the eyes of divinity, I become enchanted by the rhythm of the wind and rain. Drops of water swirl and spin around us as if they too were dancing in our moment of careless happiness. I felt my chest tighten and my heart beat faster as we drew closer together, is this what love feels like? Is this what love... and there we stood soaking wet kissing to the song of the wind and rain.

-J.P. Dumas

Sonnet XXIX: This New Zealand Land

There is no place for white poets in this New Zealand land,
So, for a people so obsessed with their own heritage,
How can you disdain where you have come from? You have come from
A world where rules were broken, not forgotten or erased.
There is no place for white poets in this New Zealand land,
There are no presses built to take my condit'nal work;
There are no people who will buy the label I was born;
'New Zealand Poet' stickers plastered over my fair skin.
But if you publish this as is, a comment on our land,
What message do you send to those who are hurt and betrayed,
For they would turn to poetry, a quite exclusive group,
And though the words would comfort them, the people there would not.
There is no place for white poets in this New Zealand land.
There is no place for me within this dark, New Zealand land.

Chris McMenamin

Floating

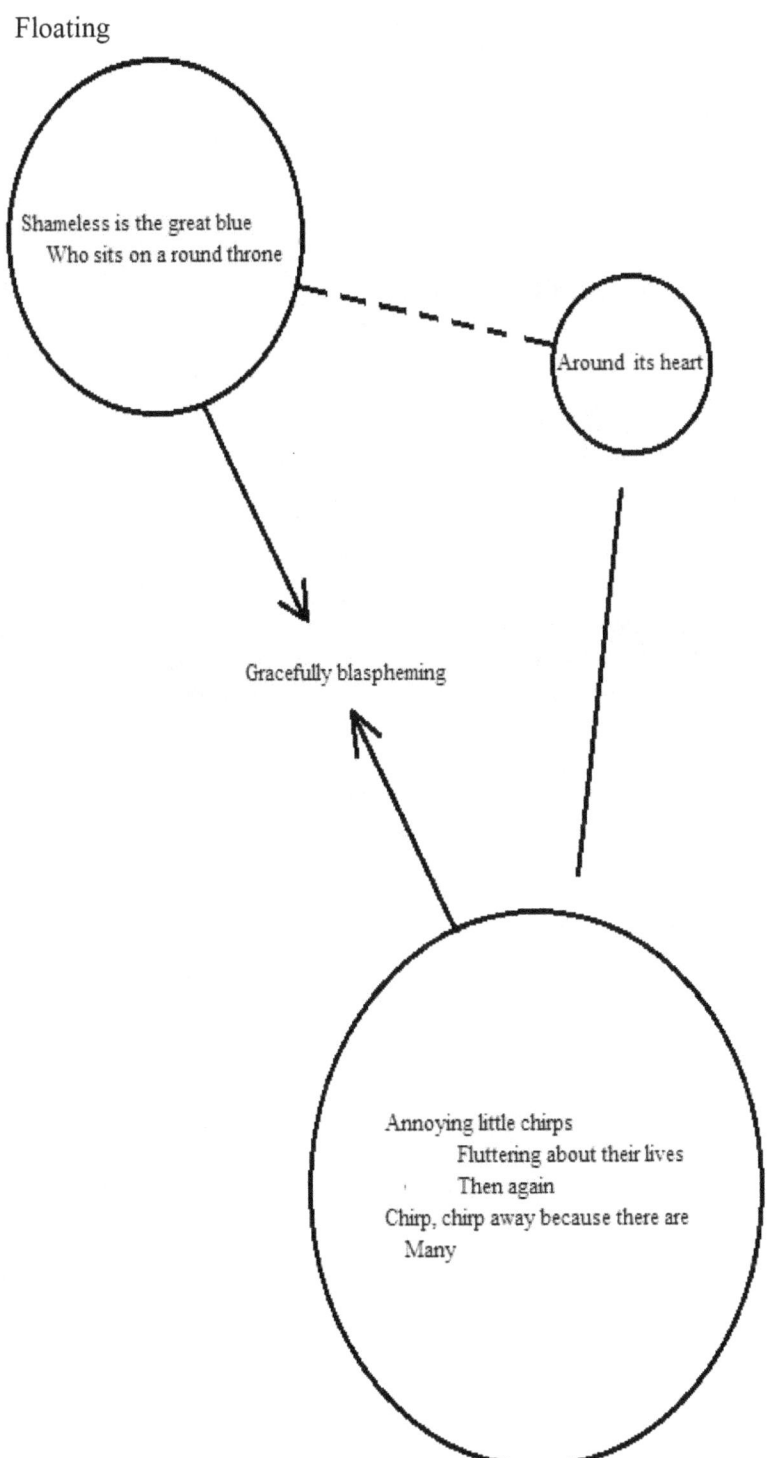

Shameless is the great blue
Who sits on a round throne

Around its heart

Gracefully blaspheming

Annoying little chirps
Fluttering about their lives
Then again
Chirp, chirp away because there are
Many

-J.P. Dumas

A Dialogue Between Pain and Self

CHORUS
The sombre scene I set before, mirrored by the clouds:
A darkened beach, storm approaching, grey mists gather 'round.
Pain and Self stand, surf and shore,
Shouting curses, nothing more.
Pain begins the dialogue, voice nasal and shrill.
Self continues on with the malicious 'ntent to kill.

PAIN
Evoke me now, lest I become, like fever, ever deadly,
For to see me now will save thee from a life yet unfulfilled,
And if I stay away, courage, thou shalt wield
For I shall increase thy tension ever read'ly.

SELF
Albeit it is true I fear an addiction of sorts.
Could a life fulfilled truly leave me so content
To never feel again? Dear Pain, give me thy dissent.

PAIN
Thou harm thyself e'er daily with such destructive thoughts.
Agony cannot be as addicting as thou say.

SELF
What of the space between the times when thou shalt strike again?
Shrinking, shrinking: 'tis thine addiction affecting me, my Pain.
If I evoke thee now, will I wait weeks, or days?

PAIN
O! Self-righteous swine! Thou sicken me! Dost thou feel no shame?!

SELF
Self-righteous? Lo! Good reason so: avoid my question not:
If I concede, how long waits I 'til agony's begot?

PAIN
It depends upon thy self-restraint, else my name be not Pain.

SELF
Thus why should not I then apply such restraint than to do as you say?

PAIN
For pressure builds and such is so: neither us shall ever go.

CHORUS
The dialogue, here, restarts now, and like the shore will ebb and flow,
Pain and Self continue so, fighting every day.
Neither victor; none resolved. Storm remaining ever.
Eternity is constant. Conflict ceases never.

Chris McMenamin

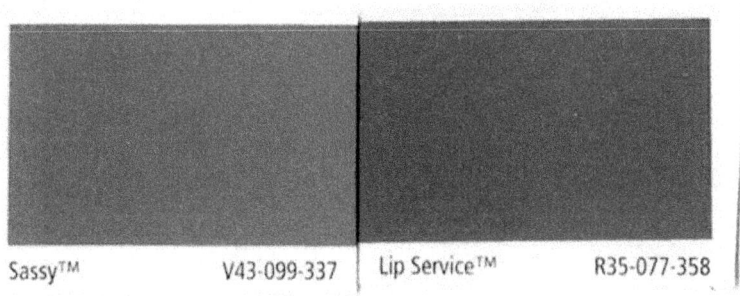

Sassy™ V43-099-337

Lip Service™ R35-077-358

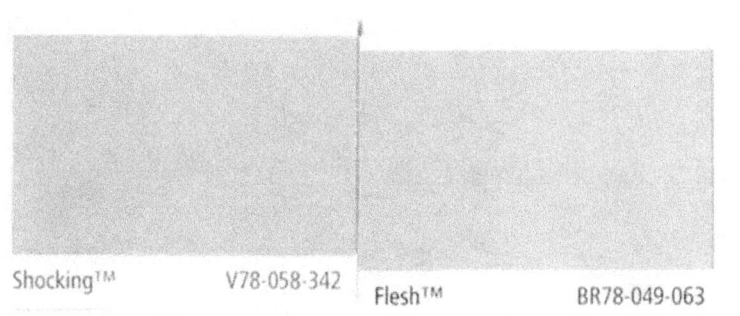

Shocking™ V78-058-342

Flesh™ BR78-049-063

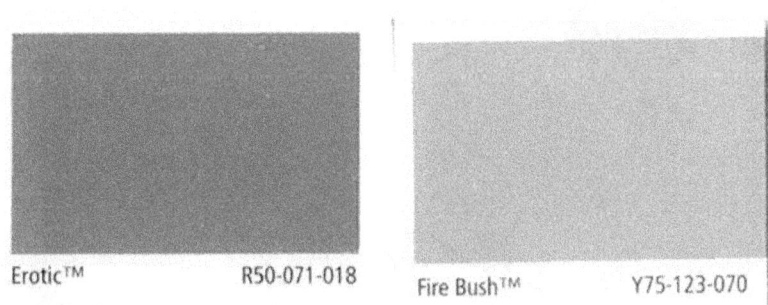

Erotic™ R50-071-018

Fire Bush™ Y75-123-070

The Nurse

Tonight she takes a different form.
A worried dream, a courting tank
German song but not to have,
And now my nurse is certain sleeping
I think the nurse has gone to bed.
Goodnight, nurse, now soaked in sweat.
Oil paint, and full of laughter.
No wonder my nurse is a-napping.
Or someone else I have at met.
She becomes a portrait dancer;
Of bustling turns and IV stabbings
Becomes, in morning, nurse once more.

Chris McMenamin

Sonnet XXII: Deareſt Roſe

The ſun, and moon, and ſtars are thine
For they are in thine eyes
Which ſoftly ſhine and twinkle;
Dancing, e'er alive.
O! If I think of all the times
I've mißed thy company,
I think I'd find I'd pray now thee
Not leave thy life, and me.
O! If amongſt the flow'rs I ſee,
I pick the deareſt rose,
It ſhall not be in ſight to thee,
Wherewith grace and repoſe.
I bid thee well as thou ſoon hie,
With tears of fervour in mine eyes.

Chris McMenamin

Red I hate you red

Red of hell, red of dreams

Of rushing and of pushing of

Dying trying

Red like crimson red like scarlet letters

Like closing eyes underwater

Waking in the night, dreaming,

Screaming

Red

SW

Memories of falling in love: Part four

"I love you."

At some point when falling in love the 'falling' ends and all you're left with is 'in love'. The moment your two orbits are so in sync every muscle in your body aches to be with the divine being of your desire. The moment you feel as if there is no you without them.

My bedroom was not the biggest, it could barely fit my bed, shelves and desk. Though that didn't matter, to us anywhere was big enough as long as it could fit us both. As we lay there kissing on my tiny bed, in my tiny room, there came a moment I realized that I would die for you, for us and for that moment in time. I knew that I loved you, there was no longer a doubt in my mind about that. "I love you". I remember your eyes tearing up as you heard those words, the truth behind them being so undeniable that they struck a chord in your soul... "I, I love you too".

-J.P. Dumas

"I am not a feminist, but I do believe in gender equality"

Sacrifice your virtue and bend your back from its bone
Men and women are enemies and he is your lucky stranger
Your hips will bare his weight without question
And your life will be chained to his merry-go-round
You will not open your womanly mouth
Or bear your womanly fruits
You will talk as small as he pleases
Because you need him
You need him
And you are nothing without him.

A back that does not bend is a back that cannot be loved
Hair that cannot be pulled
A neck that cannot be bruised
You are unfuckable with your taught bones
And your staunch spine held straight
Upon your iron body
For he is no unfitting husband among the deathless gods,
Persephone
Why are you crying out so shrilly?

Let him cuff you to his bed frame
For you are his pretty present
Let him bore into you
Tear you open
Be willing, Persephone
You are no victim here
You are in his golden chariot
And you should be so lucky

For the value of a woman depends entirely on her virtue
Men and women are enemies
But this is our un-yielding fault
As it is woman who must destroy herself to be loved

But we should all be –
So

so

lucky.

-MH

Ellie

she was strange
like me
yet everyone seemed to love her

the wind had invited me to party
and she was only in the other room

parties weren't my thing
I didn't like strangers
and I didn't know how to make small talk

so I slipped away
from the party
and found my way to a secluded music room

I sat at the piano
playing well enough to alert
a few passing strangers

not well enough for them
to actually give more than a passing glance
I played for hours
until I fell asleep

-

As I awoke
there was Ellie
she was smiling and asked
me to play another song

I told her
I wasn't really good
she said that what she heard was beautiful
Ellie was unlike
anyone I had ever met
in this faraway place

-

she spoke to me
every day after that
and dragged me along wherever she went

within months we were best friends

because of her
I began living in the real world
more than I did in my dreams

she was my anchor

something that always pulled me back
to reality
no matter how bad things got

and things got rough

-

we no longer talk

-

-J.P. Dumas

Hope's Return

Has the time / come at last / for the blossoming of spring? /
To think of all / the wasted weeks / since fate had Cupid bring /
My path into hers. / The months we could have had.

I've caught her eyes / a few times / but was never introduced; /
If I had / met her, think / of all the fun we'd have produced. /
Perhaps I shall / go forward today.

I shall miss, / when she's gone, / the falling grace of winter, /
And I fear / my love for her / will overarch the former. /
The future lies / in Hope's Return.

Chris McMenamin

at

home i

have gotten

fat i see it pools

in me in the bright

lamplightlamplight

SW

LOVE (THE BIG L)

i love this boy

with sea pebble eyes

and wind fingerprints in his hair

kissing his face smothering his cheeks

tasting breath in the air, fluttering

he is mine.

rough edges still a little unsmooth

uncaught the beams, he don't understand me when I

hold my hands to sky star-seeking eyes

call moonbeams poetry and wish on

empty water jugs

but want you to know

he is mine.

and

he loves me enough.

my love and I we boy and girl or

boys and boys or girls and girls

and the sunlight still filter through

our fingertips

the same

SW

Cunningly Lingers

Done staring

Kill living

SHE

Speaking silver

I

Existential in knowing

HE

Lingers slicker pink

Lawyers Sort
Archaic Laughing
Starting
8AM bustle
Busses clustering
Stopping there

Lively Sideways
Here you,
and me
Giving
Stopping
There

Taking is
Taking is harder
Falling
Forever
Please
Here
Forever
There
Now

Hers

Lovingly whole here

He

Flinches

She

Lingers

LONGER

She

Speaking silver

Is LONGER

Sings

LONGER

Stopping softly

She

Lovingly fuzzy

Sings

LONGER

Softly sleeps

A word

Alone

Done

Staring

Kill

Living

I speaking silver

I existential in knowing

She

Lingers slicker pink.

- MH

Sonnet XXXIII: Were Not But For This Blackened Beaſt

Were not but for this blackened beaſt which thought'ſt thou hid away,
The deadly means through which thou commit'ſt not to love thyſelf:
What gives thee life, now poiſonèd; how expect'ſt me thou tell
Thee ſole how many times I think of thee in hour, or day;
Then whole, I could preſent to you a love beyond the ſkies,
Beyond the ſpheres and viſions from a teleſcopic lens
Where conſtancy, my dedication, is my lone offenſe
(O! ſhould I then not her endow and with friends her baptiſe?).
Yet it is here, this beaſt, and I cannot extend my love.
What weathered chance that fate would ever thus allow withal?
Thus leaving me with none for love yet one I can enthrall
In Fate's conqueſt: my ſword in hand, and hand in Cupid's glove.
Such words I ſay again, again, until I know them right:
Were not but for this blackened beaſt, I would love thee tonight.

Chris McMenamin

OUT

OUT –

Not more, no more and –

RUN –

Take the bedclothes, cast them

OUT –

Someplace –

He'll never come back.

OUT –

Since yesterday and who the hell

Needed him anyway –

No more –

Goddamn cricket

Coffee cups and insidious stains –

Chuck OUT –

His goddamn shoes and his goddamn neckties

Strangle him – and her –

Let him writhe in perfect misery

NO ONE and
No toothbrush.

Going OUT –

Don’t spill the milk

Make the tea

Put on the dress, dab on the rouge

Better this way.

OUT –

Going OUT –

Back to the supermarket.

Now

Get the rice thing and the full cream and

The cat treats.

SW

Habitual Misery

Fall into a habit
Of euphoria and bliss
And watch those around you;
It's you that they miss.

You've gone from this world
Yet your corpse lives behind:
Marred, burned, and scarred,
And lacking a mind.

A sigh of desire
As the bags 'round my eyes
Force me to a world of
Illusions and lies.

My dreams linger on,
O! the happiest place,
Where true peace of mind
Is winning the race.

But all dreams must end
With the sunrise;
Your lack of soul shows
Through the tears in your eyes.

Chris McMenamin

Memories of falling in love: Part one

"First kiss."

I recently found myself reminiscing on what it felt like to fall in love. I remember there being this sort of other worldliness to the "first kiss" that initial leap into the unknown reaches of another's soul. That moment in which the whole world goes quiet no matter where you are, as if the entire universe is holding its breath waiting to see two souls collide. Followed shortly by an explosion of ecstatic emotion. The moments after being equally as beautiful, filled with giggles, smiles and cuddles. Simply put, magical.

-J.P. Dumas

Sonnet XXIII: His Lady

His lady is a bottle, sold by solitude.
He nurses at his lady's breast as though it gives him life.
His numbered days, though limited, hold his drink ever rife.
Ne'er should he be alone, for lady, or for lassitude
Stand watch over his bloodless corpse as sentries keeping guard
Over a sanguine prisoner, sent'nced by his own accord.
Weaning from one bottle t'find another in his ward;
His lady not a bottle, but emotion ever marred.
His lady calls him softly. His lady sings his name.
His lady doth find relish in the comfort of his drink,
In the desire she provides, evermore aflame,
As she retains any reason for him to ever think.
His lady is a bottle, sold by solitude.
He hides within his bottle, sealed by habitude.

Chris McMenamin

skinny white woman

weaves her hair through her hair with her
underwear on backwards insides out
who made underwear anyway

life is nicer
without breeches pantyhose drop the bloomers
so why can't she drop the panty

she sings this song while bending down
white ribcage he calls out
but she absorbed on the cotton thread, so small
pulling pulling out her underwear she should pull it
she could go naked out the door, run, sprinting

then what would they think

SW

In the BEDROOM

Fat MAN like BURNING water on her thigh

TEASES pooling into TEASES/pooling into

BOLD

She was BOLD.

In the shower

Fat ran like wrinkled water on her thigh

Creases pooling into creases/pooling into

Old

She was old.

SW

a poem to that wall

once i saw you smoking against that wall
i never liked it when you smoked
i could never breathe around you
anyway

you haven't touched that wall in years
you probably don't remember seeing me there
i was late for a lecture
in a language you don't know

you still smoke, of course, or, at least, i assume,
yet you haven't touched
that
wall since

once i saw you walking with spaghetti
in your mind
and on your lips
you had something else on both as well

when another smoker-on-the-wall my way came
what was i do to
but to say yes
always yes

chris mcmenamin

THE MAGIC DRAWER

CoME oNE!

CoME aLL

To SeE ThE wonDers oF thE DraWer

ClOSe YoUr EyEs aNd MaKE a WiSh

The DraWer caN GrAnt it!

As LonG

As YoU RembeR ThESe WoRDs…

STRAWBERRY JAM!

EvRy One KnOws

ThE Drawer wAnTS YOU to fEeL SaFe…

-J.P. Dumas

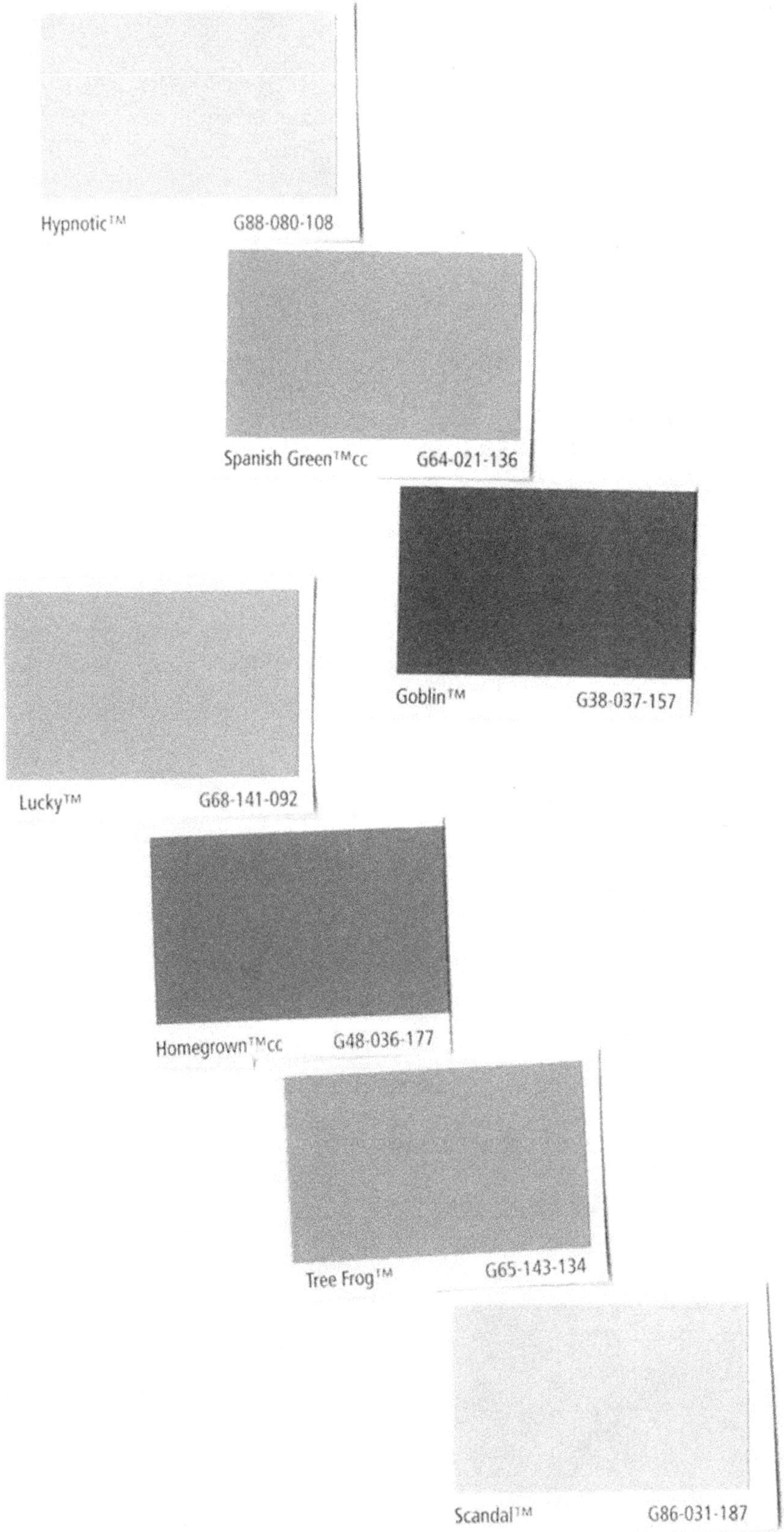
Hypnotic™ G88-080-108
Spanish Green™cc G64-021-136
Goblin™ G38-037-157
Lucky™ G68-141-092
Homegrown™cc G48-036-177
Tree Frog™ G65-143-134
Scandal™ G86-031-187

The Trees

Above the canopies
Bend like humbled monks
So fresh so green
So old so ancient
Chapel made of earth

Below
Blackened roots drink
The water fill the emptiness of
The soil reach
Down down

Follow the stems up
The trunk to branches reaching to the sky
To leaves -
Surpass song surpass breath
Reach to the sky
Like a prayer

SW

Message from the Sea

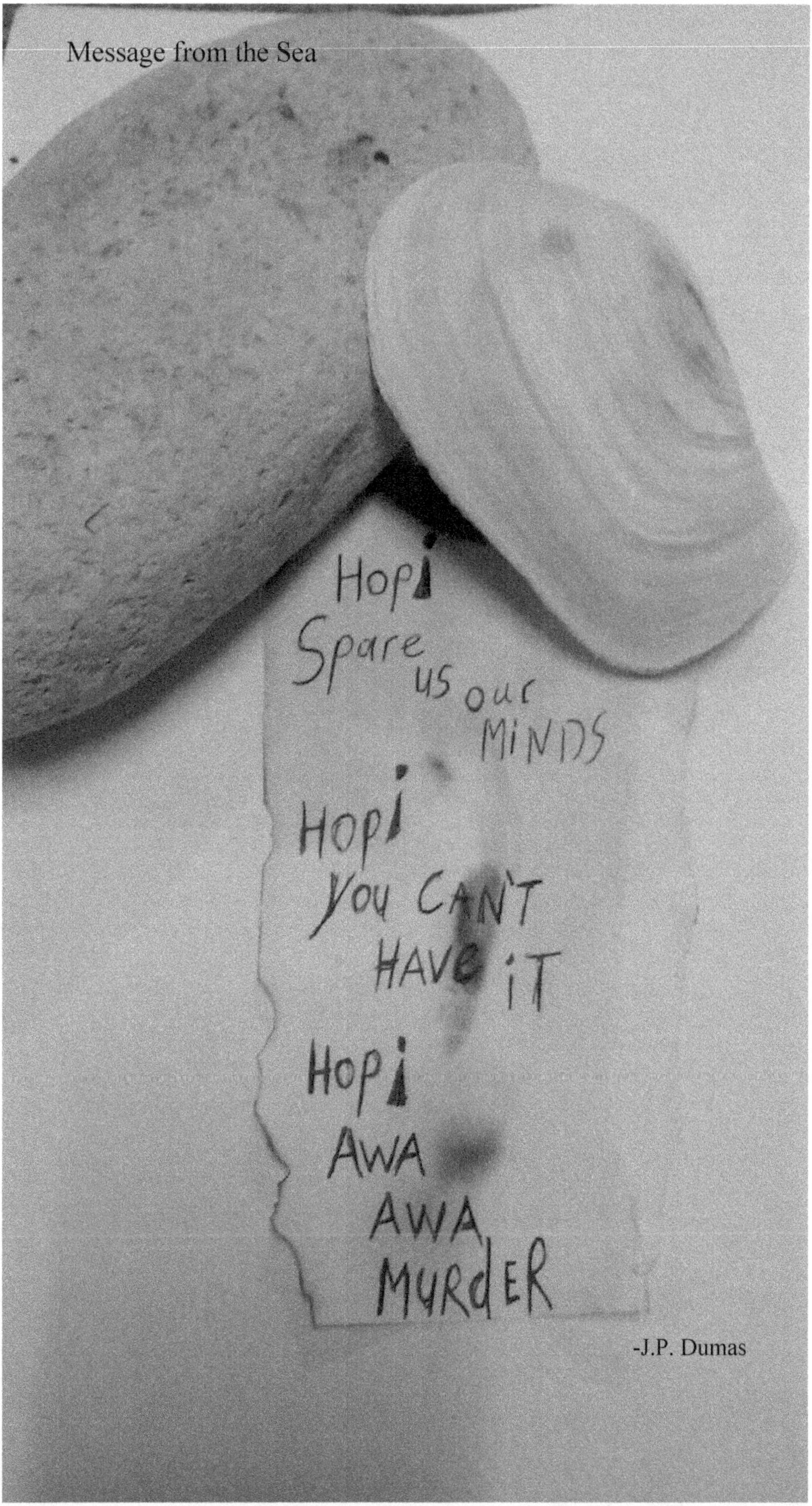
Hopi
Spare us our
MINDS
Hopi
You CAN'T
HAVE iT
Hopi
AWA
AWA
MURdER

-J.P. Dumas

The Grimm Sonnets

I
Chiming Bone

Blood-stained stones that form a bridge, a boar lying atop.
Enchanted spear is misplaced near the bank where brother's lain.
The man who walks does walk away, proclaims: the beast is slain!
In public he will mourn his loss, in private he will stop.

A shepherd finds an exposed bone with such a polished shine,
He brings it to his rustic home and gives it to his wife.
His wife drills holes into the bone and makes a tuneful fife.
When brought to face, before one plays, the instrument does chime:

Dear sir, you blow upon my bone, so I give you my thanks.
My brother struck me dead and now I am not yet at rest.
To win a wife, both he and I uptook her father's quest
To kill a boar, which I did do, and now lie underbank.

The bone to king, the king to man, the man to bridge again.
Now brother's drownèd for his crimes, the king cries: beast is slain!

II
Finding Fear

A phantom lingers in the belfry: sexton dressed in white.
A boy who rings the bells gives warning and is not afraid.
His second warning and his third do naught to ghost persuade.
The sexton at the staircase-foot lives luckily tonight.

Beneath the gallows sit seven fellows once wed to air, now floor.
On and on the fire flickers; now their trousers burn.
Compassion made him cut them down, now with a voice so stern:
"If you don't watch your trousers catch, I'll hang you up once more!"

In a castle filled with ghosts and demon-animals,
His skills, though few, are put to use to play such silly sports.
The spirits there all leave at twelve and so cut his fun short.
A wife is what the boy had found, but still not fear at all.

So while he slept, his wife then crept down to the palace lake.
With fish and water in his bed, the prince began to shake!

III

Lamb's Lettuce

A mother views the house next-door and gazes from her sill.
She looks upon the Lamb's Lettuce and thinks she'll surely die.
Her husband vows protection and thus to the garden pries:
He steals the herb the she desires: its name is Rapunzel.

The child's claimed by witch-next-door who acts as child's mother.
She's named after the garden-jewel and loved for every day
Until the age of twelve when she is then taken away.
Rapunzel now lives in safety locked in a secret tower.

A prince now finds her all alone "Rapunzel, let your hair
Fall from this your tower so that I may climb atop."
The girl now falls in love and yet the witch with her does swap
And gauges out the prince's eyes; sends her from prince's care.

And now they meet in wilderness amid their joinèd fears:
The prince's eyes are healèd by Rapunzel's mother-tears.

IV
The Moon

Four businessmen once left their town to escape night-darkness.
In three towns over was an orb so bright they could see by.
A nearby farmer answered "that's the moon up in our sky."
The businessmen then took it home where it would luminesce.

The mayor paid them three talents for bringing him the moon.
The townspeople gave them a coin each week as like a fine
For trimming wick, filling oil, and maintaining its shine.
When the men died, a quarter each was placed in each man's tomb.

The moon reassembled itself in once-dark underworld.
The dead began to reawake and drink and dance in clubs.
Saint Peter came and yelled at them and then, just as abrupt,
He stole the moon and hung it up for the entire world.

He takes a portion every week and puts it back each month.
He does this so moon's ownership is questioned by no one.

Chris McMenamin

Blade of the earth

Come, blade of the earth, umhlaba
That the heavens gave us, izulu
That we can gather wood from the trees,
izihlahla

That we can create fire, umlilo
Come, blade of the earth, umhlaba
To keep us warm, afudumele
To fill our bellies.
Ithemba

Come, blade of the earth, ukubulala
That the heavens gave us, isihogo
That we can break the steel from our chains,
ngozankosi

That we can feel free, ukufa
Come, blade of the earth, ukubulala
To end this life, ukuphila
To bring us hope.
Ithemba

J.P. Dumas

NOVE FIORI

CHRIS MCMENAMIN

Running wildly into a forest of strange words…

L'origine del senso

UMANA!

Tutti i nostri parenti con cui abbiamo

UMANA!

Cosi, a dispetto fermezza…

UMANA!

Somiglianze

Di sotto

Quella

Tra noi che un tempo

Scendendo terra

UMANA!

TERRA!

FOSSILE!

-J.P. Dumas

The Labyrinth V: From moss co'ered walls, I walk away

I

From moss-co'ered walls, I walk away
Into the charrèd, humming sea,
Where I remain and rest my days;
O! Labyrinth, how I miss thee!

II

And in the constant rumble-hiss,
No shades have, to me, themselves shown,
Nor met me with a humble kiss:
Sans memories, I'm one alone.

III

But since I met that wretched shade
For whom I care so deep, yea! fond,
Perhaps I best rewalk path made
By love, and with that love, abscond.

IV

So fall in love again, shall I,
To live upon this lovely path,
For know I, love shall never die,
But conquer hearts with its own wrath.

Chris McMenamin

Babylon

Babylon alone knows where my heart will find its best.
Babylon alone will see me find the lightened life.
Babylon alone knows where I will spend my day.

The muted orange is broken
by a bed of green on which
lies a sea of deep purple
orchids and irises.
My final resting place
stretches far over
the asperous desertscape.
I reach to touch the grass.
The grass sighs in response.
The wind has subsided,
and the course needles
have been replaced
by loving kisses.
The grass tickles my callouses,
my knees, my face.
I water the garden
with grateful tears.
The orchids fasten themselves
to my nose—
scentless by nature;
natural by scent—
and are plastered in my hands:
petals alight against
the black-yellow setting sun.
A single hour sets the sun
with its compassion
and behind me dawns
a new light.

A mountain
stands before my eyes,
lit by beads of light
unimaginably attained,
in four grand tiers.
The colours!
I walk toward the mountain,
and as I near it, I see.
On the first tier
of the mountain,
bushes of fine-leaved peonies,
bursting with brilliant reds.
The second, a myriad of apple
trees, bearing bright flowers,
and rich red fruit;
pink apocynums decorating
the vines uphanging.
The third, tiger lilies enflaming
the trunk of
the date-plum trees.
On the fourth tier hangs
powder-yellow Pyrenean lilies.
Atop the mountain,
almost invisible, are fruit trees
of every sort;
the channels descending
the mountain are flowing
with clear water.

My lips are dry
and my stomach quivers.
I step toward
the mountain to touch—
marble!
I grope the peonies
and begin to circulate
the mountain,
finding after a short while
an archway of reeds.
Across the threshold
is the interior of the mountain.
The room smells of
sandalwood and rose.
Inside, a consortium of mirrors
centred
around a group of
candles in such a way
that it
illuminates
the entire structure.
I move toward the candles,
yellow beeswax—
they smell like
yellow beeswax—
and in the
mirrors I see
myself.

Babylon alone knows where my heart will ever rest.
Babylon alone will see me sleep on purple cot.
Babylon alone knows where my head will final lay.

Chris McMenamin

Flowers bite back

Have you ever closed your eyes,
held your breath and ran headlong into certain doom?

I have.

Weeks spent rolling around in meadows of white petals
lead to such ecstatic hopefulness.

I was blinded to my intrusion
upon the land where flowers grew.

The more I became entranced by the heavenly scent,
the closer I came to

— the rows of white roses —

Until I slipped and fell.

As I tried to claw my way out thorns tore at me,
each one exposing my weakness more and more.

Finally collapsing.

The sweet stings lulled me to sleep.

At least the roses can grow now, wild and free.

-J.P. Dumas

Notes on flowers and dreams

Dreams, no, gorgeous nightmares fill my mind whenever I close my eyes. I see joy, beauty and happiness for myself and for flowers. Yes, flowers! I'm sure it's a metaphor for something... I hate the fact that I am happier when my eyes are closed than I am when they are open, because when I wake up I realize that my dreams are just that: dreams. My soul is stripped bare and my heart shattered.Dreams, beautiful and treacherous.

-J.P. Dumas

Green I want you green

Green of daylight rising, green of

Bud unfurled and the end

Of the rain.

Green

Under the soil, under the surface,

Brittle, breakable,

Still a small thing, still

Leaf palms stretching

To the sun

SW

How does the tangerine taste?
With first, a seasoned, piquant bite.
A hesitance... and something else?
And something older. Byzantine.

And tell me then of other fruits.
Of plums and peaches, how do they taste?
I taste their plucking from the branch.
I taste their pleasant stone-fruit flesh.

And tell me of the taste of the spanish lime
Which lingers on the tongue like vanished time.
Or lemons. Which feel like the whole world
When tasted in French.

Chris McMenamin

A garden on the ground

-J.P. Dumas

naked skin and hair like madame butterfly

tell me of a house
with sand zen gardens
and cross-stitched fruit
you ask
and i say

the yellow is mine by now
unless my sister is in there
there is no physician to imprison me here
on this mat on a wooden floor
the light is a different world
a paper globe
the pattern on the wall zigs and zags and is broken
by fingernail scratches
from bunkbeds where teeth went through lips
the corner by the wardrobe was a good hiding place
i was still small enough
fur elise plays on that wooden train
from the salvation army store
a novelty, i know
a stained-glass paper cross on the window
with the lord's prayer
obfuscated
by those thick
vertical bars of green

|threshold|

black and white
a cow in corner
chessboard tiles
door panels black and white
those window slates there can be removed

|threshold|

look up
you can see the attic
you just can't
reach
look past the rainbow dolphins
glimpse your reflection
in the black-and-white room

|threshold|

burns your feet
return to the yellow sanctuary for socks
king arthur's table and curtains—tulips—
green and pink and blue
there's a lip on the floor
don't stub your toe
dutch houses everywhere
clogs
a flying man with goggles
don't stub your toe
by god
don't stub your toe

|threshold|

i used to have that one
it's bigger than mine
of course
but now he's put a black panther manifesto on the
door
i don't understand

opposite the front door
with the different coloured glass
panels
is a contortion of limbs
and naked skin
and hair like madame butterfly
with green nails
she is grafted to the tree

|threshold|

what of the room out back
you ask
did you meet a lady there
perhaps
once
you ask
let's go back inside
i say
and shut the way
the door
and not come back
i say
i need to go to sleep
i say
i haven't slept much recently
tonight won't be any different
i think but do not say
i just want you to
go away
i think but do not say

|threshold|

so you ask
tell me of a house
with sand zen gardens
and cross-stitched fruit
and i say
i don't remember much
i don't remember much
i say

Chris McMenamin

Dry Leaves

Stepping on dry leaves
Brings our cruel smiles wider
And pain to the leaves.

*

We let the leaves lie
In pieces on the concrete.
These are not our leaves.

*

New leaves will soon fall
From a branch which will not heal.
More leaves will soon break.

Chris McMenamin

Mm what a lovely green tree

- mh

When Lorca Speaks of Bells

Why does

The imagining

Of sunken bells

Deep in green seas

Of seaweed

Fill my mind like chocolate

A tongue

But not quite

I think it is because I like chocolate

But far better still

Is the taste unknown

The bells submerged

The ancient depths

The song I wish to hear

Because

It cannot possibly

Be sung

SW

con la morte della mia anima
he tells himself a red panda
since he sees russet markings
on his soul and on his skin
c'è una nuova gioia
a rising from the ashes
la luce prospera nel buio
its white-gold glowing
assured in its own
markings he saw
e poi il diavolo macchiato
sullen liar
apologised
piangendo per la sua perdita
of a detuned piano
weeping a ragtime
composition of accidental
violence
portato sfiga sui suoi nemici
he finds solitude in the water

Chris M

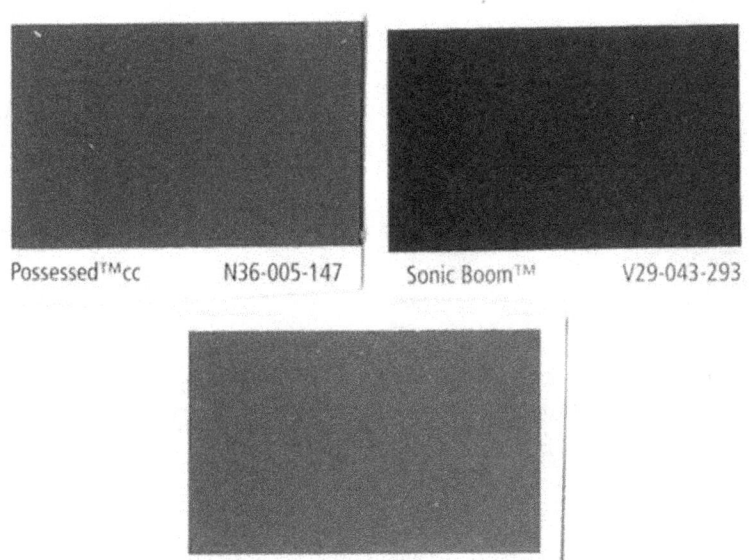

Possessed™cc N36-005-147

Sonic Boom™ V29-043-293

Warlord™cc V40-019-295

Tonys Pink™ 077-064-040

Indian Ink™cc B26-017-270

A CLASS

Narration. Speaking faster to hear the knowledge, not slowing time but speeding it. Red it's a colour. It's a colour on top of other colours. It's a colour that doesn't help the Knowledge flow but yet it is there, on top of the knowledge. I wonder If Time helps knowledge, Time is Knowledge? How does the Knowledge reach the box. The Box That Holds The Knowledge. The Box is under the space and the space flows. The Sun is Too Bright. The Sun, the suns, there are so many suns in Space. So many suns they almost hide the knowledge. Green, Green, Greens and the fountains are behind The Knowledge. A Fisher to both sides of the knowledge but it's not a fisher like the fisher on the beach. It's a fisher that indicates where to find The Knowledge. It isn't hard to find the knowledge. It's there, Right there under the red, but finding space in the box that is the trick.

-J.P. Dumas

Elegy: Scores of Weeks

I

Scores of weeks since have gone past that I waited for my love to return, / 'las she is gone from my life. As, for a new love, I yearn.

II

Yet after years I have sought you, new love, who is less fair than no-one. / Within each shining blonde hair, hideth a ray of the sun.

III

Now, I must find comfort where I will go; know I, thou wilt not love me. / Farewell to trust and to thee: This is my trust's elegy.

CHRIS McMENAMIN

Memories of falling in love: Part three

"Late nights and long calls."

It's strange, when falling in love there is this continuous urge to be in one another's presence. Atoms drawn to each other, every fibre of your being calling out into space hoping for an echo.

I remember sitting by my phone drinking my third cup of coffee because I didn't want to be asleep when you called, if you called. The moment my phone lit up with your number was like a sunrise at 11pm. We would spend hours after that talking about everything and nothing at the same time. It wasn't about the conversation it was about feeling close to you. When I closed my eyes the miles between us disappeared and you were right there next to me. So we whispered sweet nothings to each other until neither of us could keep our eyes open and as sleep overcame me, I could feel your soul right there next to mine.

-J.P. Dumas

Unconditional

I will be with you
No matter where you go
Or what you do.

I will support and aid
And be with you
Through light and shade

Until the day
When my light fades.
Do not feel dismay

For I will be,
In every way,
With you, see?

I will be each drop of sun.
I will be each brilliant tree.
I will be, with nature, one.

– CM

The Labyrinth I: Enter I, in twisted path

I

Enter I, in twisted path
To hide or face these terror-dreams.
Walk I, now, this solemn space
For fear of those recurring themes.

II

Mem'ries, both those sour, and sweet,
Enter mind, each step I take.
To know which mem'ries to fare well,
Such memories I first must wake.

III

Haunting; else words can't describe
The presence of ones I knew well
Who whisper wicked things to me:
Yet 'tis my voice, and self I tell.

IV

Ay, centre now, I do arrive,
And centre-piece, I see.
I banish fear, and leave it there
For all eternity.

Chris McMenamin

Empty Red

Raise Me
To The
Light

and Let this hand
guide you *Trough*
The Empty
Red

FOLLOW
THE
RED
IT NEEDS
TO
TRUST

ALL
IN
TIME

For her Dreams
are
greater
STiLL

and Mine
Fade
with
Her

-J.P. Dumas

The light from the fridge reveals all midnight snacking
The chocolate hidden in the veggie drawer
A persimmon from in the butter shelf
A scoffing of the juice like bottled port

The light from the fridge reveals all midnight snacking
Sneaky brownie with leftover cream
Why are barley sugars in the fridge
The talcum powder memories flooding back

The light from the fridge reveals all midnight snacking
A gorging of the times she was alive
They say that talc might cause cancer you know
Better stick with the chocolate in the veggie draw then

Chris McMenamin

A Dialogue Between My Love and Me

Upon the snow-capped mountains, I converse with my love.
I see the mountain's harmony: the settled snow, the bated breeze,
And her and I standing atop; I see my lady blush.
Though I speak first, the dialogue was first started by she.

Say I, "'tis sole a travesty to give myself to thee
Lest thou in bravest courage prove and give thyself to me."
Says she, "ay, but in thy tender love, experience resides:
A means through which"—she takes a breath—"thou would force me to die."

"You mislead thyself and self-deceive", say I, "if that is thy belief.
A flatt'ring thought, but 'tis thy move, for I, for sure, shan't lead."
Says she. "That's fine with all of me", and looks into mine eye;
"I act! Put self, or shut thy mouth!" Say I nothing, but sigh.

The wind; it howls. It speaks my pain. It evokes tears from me.
The rage is fuelled by my own love, and heated snow is caused by she.
Have I disturbed this harmony and angered this, now bitter, breeze?
The mountain says that man must love; says that it once made me.

So I, in humble protest speak; my speech that doth emerge
Is contr'ry to th'intended mean: I cannot find the words I need.
Now bare, she stands in front of me, her bare words seek assent.
I speak. I mean to disagree, but do relent and thus consent.

And then I said "I liked it so." Her lips spoke lonesome letters, "no."
The mount has told me what to love. I shan't dissent but sadly show.
The elements have ravished me: my love controls the wind and snow.
I stand as idol for the man who will dissent, then sadly show.

Chris McMenamin

Bumper Sticker Theology

Here is a truth that reaches into the deepest
part of what it is to be a person
if we are faithful to him here
"here" does not mean that it is not
real or that it is not in this world
A kingdom of
darkness is here, certainly
"evil" is very much here to be
Feared
The "enemies" are
certainly here like
here is the dining room

as long as we humans have been here
soft wriggle underfoot there/ a silky massage
there
we are free - for now
here a scratching shouder/ can't reach here/

some degree of control over things is now
recognized – flinch
now what can we do – whir
even now – guttural growl
now gods own kingdom - cogs
where it is now excluded – a sticky tear
now widely misunderstood – there
now the whole earth is full of his glory – blade
through my side
and now the same life flows –
grinding/gnawing/grating

think now of the barcodes used in most stores –
grating bones/ grating bones
life now being lived has no necessary
connection – gushing blood
but now let us try out a subversive thought – a
sticky tear/a sticky waterfall of orange dewy
tears
solutions to problems that now seem
unsolvable – a blade through my side
Life, our actual existence, is not included in
what is now – a blade through my lung

A pool

of dark ochre – bones askew
a punctured lung – a broken spine – floating

– in a pool of orange dewy tears.

- MH

WRITER'S BLOCK

do something, else, drink tea, walk
walk the dog, drink milk, walk, now
to bedroom, plant flower, do, not i
repeat, I, cannot, ever, write, at, all

SW

Grace

The church burns down.
Neither accident, not arson,
Left alone to burn
In the ruins of itself.

A black-veil'd woman
Stands there to watch
The misery burning
On the dreams of others.

Rain falls
And feeds the fire
As water streams
Down her face.

The Shades climb the walls,
Their shadows, though black,
Show through the fire
And through the veil.

Chris M

Lonely on metal rock

Little stars scatter around

It just sits there on its chair

Dreadfully alone, wishing it was still one of those stars

Filled with the great BOOM of the universe

Yet it isn't, it's here

On the ground surrounded by empty souls

All sitting in one place staring at their own stars

Dreaming of the BANG

the Bang

the bang

Wasted. Beautiful. Alone.

-J.P. Dumas

Sonnet V: Night's Revenge

I dug my claws into her
To never let her go,
But before I ever did,
Her self, to I, did show.
I retracted them because I knew
She wasn't right for me.
My claws left scratches, scars, and cuts;
My claws left me to flee.
Though so much time has passed,
I feel guilt for all the pain.
I tell myself, though I know it false,
It shall never happen again.
I bade her, once, goodbye.
Her first and last goodbye.

Chris McMenamin

A list of statements to try on a coffee date

"Do you understand what it means to truly be alive? It's to feel the soul of the world around you."

"There comes a time in every person's life where they feel like they are on the edge of a cliff, sometimes it's best to let go and see what happens."

"People get weird when I talk about sex, I don't understand why? Sex is just a part of being human… a particularly good part."

"I love dancing! There is something about the motion, the intimacy… It's simply extraordinary."

"I feel like there is a certain wonder to the way each person walks, a unique stomp of being if you will."

"Senses are such a strange thing… Take smell for instance, it seems simple yet we use it to find love."

"I do so enjoy closing my eyes and drifting off into the void of my mind, strange visions and dreams are great forms of entertainment."

-J.P. Dumas

Doomed

The imperfections you can see
Mean nothing whatsoe'er to me.
I see beauty, strength, and pride,
You see reason to run and hide.

Cry in secret, I will too.
Together we will pull you through.
Burns will heal and scars will fade,
Together we'll stop that tear cascade.

If fate decrees it not to be,
It appears you soon shall part.
But stay with me, 'gainst destiny
And we shall make a start.

Alas today, Dido I play,
With her sword in her hand.
But I won't run away
When we meet in Hades' land.

Instead I shall embrace;
My death was not your fault.
While in my face, this barren place,
Your true self I exalt.

Chris McMenamin

Little Wanderer

Red door opens to a wide space to the sounds of family

The tiles are *cold* beneath my feet It's a good cold because the house is warm Warm everything about it was warm It was so warm that daddy would sometimes sleep on the couch

Across the room stood another door this door led to the grey place

The grey place was warm too but it was outside BEHIND me the smell of fresh baked bread It was warm There wasn't *a door* between the smell and me only an *archway* leading to it

the room with the smeLL was smaller and the tiles still cooled my feet there was so much Light and warmth then the Dark square behind it *Another archway*

It led to a small space in the middle of all the other spaces It was cold here and there was only one little light I came here to hide from the noise and the warmth

Bright lights outside made me run to this space and hide in its cool embrace It was safe There were

Four doors leading from this space

Glass door led to the biggest space It was *warmer* than all the rest

Carpets made it even *warmer*

in the corner a fire burned in a sea rock fire place surrounding it was mural dedicated to the place the rocks were stolen from the towering rocks made it almost to the roof and on top

a lighthouse

This room was also **very loud** Yelling was always in this room

the Clang of wedding rings against the towering rocks

Ships ignoring the lighthouse

No

Back through the glass to the small space

the grey door in the middle led to nowhere special It was an average room

The room did make a lot of noise I was scared of it sometimes other things were Scarier and

I'd hide in the loud room Under the bed the wooden floors were cool The *purrs* of cats were warm They liked to hide here too

This is also the room were the Men in White ran to I think there was a Monster in the closet

I liked hiding in the small room more The next door was big and it led to the bathroom The smell of soap and steam was warm The marble floors were cold very cold
In the corner stood a great bath with golden claWs

I liked taking bathes in it But sometimes daddy would take very Long

sometimes it was loud too Mostly when I let in the Puppies through the window Mummy didn't want them inside She didn't want Mud on the carpets
It wasn't fair the kitties could come inside and purr their *warm purrs*

so I'd hide in the small room with the Puppies The last
door had wheels and it made Space Noises That was
my first room I put all my Toys in it

Daddy even let me play on his computer I liked playing on it
I pretended It was my spaceship and all the warmth and noise couldn't
get through My Super Space Door

It also had a window Big enough for the *Puppies!* So when the noise
would stop I could sneak them inside It had another door
Big and wooden like the bathroom

That one led to the second biggest room

My second room!

This is the one where I'd sleep although it wasn't Safe
I could hear all the noise It was cool though It had Stone tiles
that were very Old But I could hear everything

It was always so **very loud**

I miss the noise

Now it's just quiet Rather a far
away

Memory

-JP Dumas

My Sin™ Y80-148-072

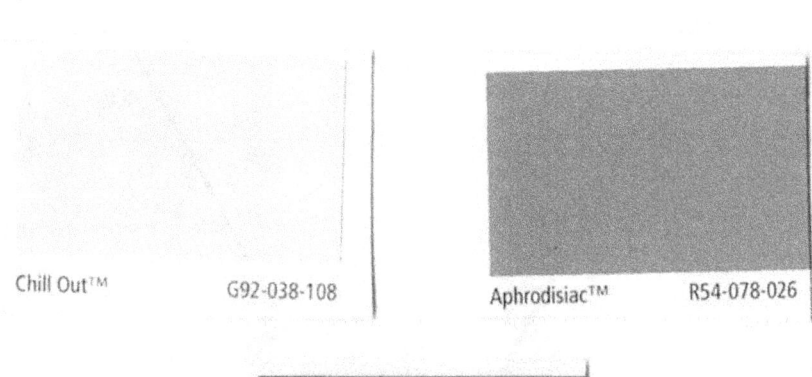

Chill Out™ G92-038-108

Aphrodisiac™ R54-078-026

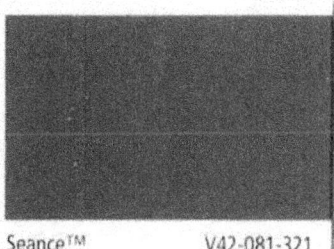

Seance™ V42-081-321

Drawing in the sky

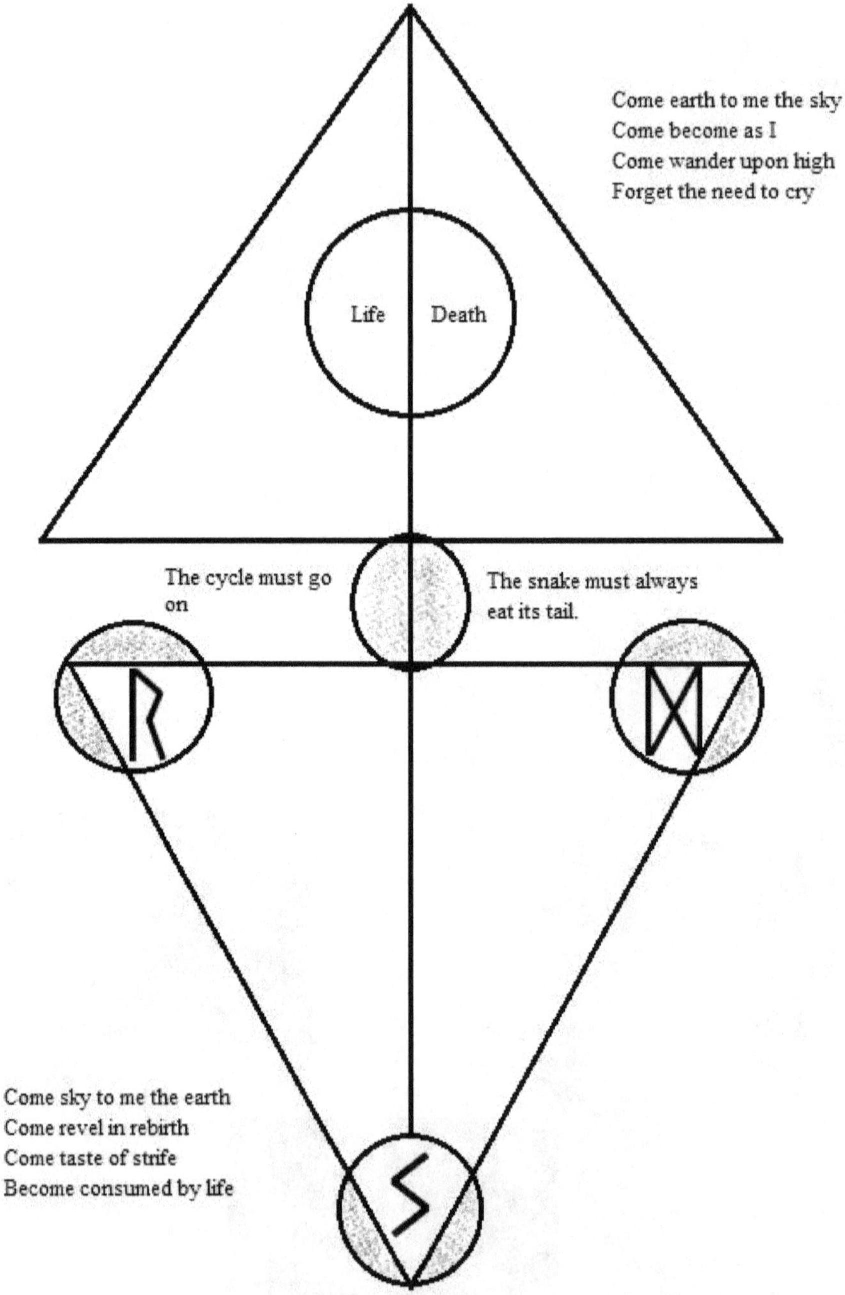
Come earth to me the sky
Come become as I
Come wander upon high
Forget the need to cry
Life
Death
The cycle must go on
The snake must always eat its tail.
Come sky to me the earth
Come revel in rebirth
Come taste of strife
Become consumed by life

-J.P. Dumas

DOWN WITH ME
down with
me
we swear
now that
the mangled
scars
are but traces of warmth
feel
shattered
weary
crippled
mad.
it does seem
at last
still
on the other side.
Falling.
struggle
Waiting.
softly hear him
call
and
silence
now.

Chris McMenamin

Poem

It was late and I said

we were on a break

as I threw you against the wall
smashed the sugared façade of your words like
long sought for wells, pulled up run dry –
I said it was over and
maybe we were better as
friends on Facebook, who saw each other
now and again
I was giving you up, like one gives up
fad diets and bad shows on the TV
it was me, not you,
I was over it, I didn't see
the point –
you didn't offer me anything
didn't complete me anyway -

forgive me,

poem,

I did not mean it.

SW

I am a locked box

I am a locked box.

A cluster of timid taste buds clinging to rooftops
A swallow of pre-loved air for extra time

Ache amongst ribs
Yawn amongst friends
Last second lessons
Emails unanswered

Glass shrieks underfoot
A kettle cries –
I cant deny I have feelings for you.

Measured canyons

between thighs

On badly patterned seats –

This will be the last time.

-MH

Quick before they are gone

What do you really want?
Why does a lady have lavender?
Where am I?
I am a locked box?
Misery knowing not…
The pleasure of grabbing words from the sky.
I need to go for a walk
Get out more often.

-J.P. Dumas

Mia.

I once knew a young woman named Mia.
Stones were thrown at her window and she answered each call
With a warm smile and a warmer embrace.

I once knew a young woman named Mia.
She noticed not the miniscule fissures forming in her glass heart
And carried on with warmth and passion.

I once knew a young woman named Mia.
She chose to ignore the cracks growing in her window,
Claiming they were not worth her worry.

There once was a young woman named Mia.
She lay on her bed, blood streaming from her face
As the shattered window covered every inch of her being.

I once met a young woman named Mia.
She met me and used me as a window frame
To rebuild her life.

I once knew a young woman named Mia.
Stones were thrown through her empty frame and she glared
With a cold grimace and a colder heart.

There once was a young woman named Mia.
She had no frame to use, no passions to love.
She had not herself, nor friends, nor even family.

I once knew a young woman named Mia.
She was unnoticed, unappreciated, and fragile.
She was glass.

There once was a young woman named Mia.

Chris McMenamin

Poetry Girl

You know what she said but you've forgotten how.
You seem to think it is quite redundant now.
You know how she felt, or so you'll admit.
Your Poetry Girl,
This is how she said it:

She wrote you fourteen lines and cited them all.
She wrote a couplet in lipstick on the wall.
As she spoke each word, she stared into your eyes.
Your Poetry Girl:
Your lows and your highs.

And she whispered it in the dark of the night:
A comfort to tell her all will be alright.
Though you never said it, she heard it, it seems.
Your Poetry Girl:
The girl of your dreams.

Then she shouted it out from up on the hill
When all you wanted was for her to be still
And take in the sunset and the changing hue.
She got what she wanted;
She got it from you.

She told you she loved you like she had before.
She said she loved you as if there were more.
She carved it, and drew it, and made it her song.
Your Poetry Girl,
So long. So long.

CHRIS McMENAMIN

Sonnet XXXVII: His Callouſed Hands Were Juſt the Start

His callouſed hands were juſt the ſtart of his grand collection of ſcars
And when I aſked to feel his hands, I felt the other ſcars there too.
I felt thoſe ſcars' proud hiſtories: the hand that clutched thoſe broken ſhards
Of glaß, thoſe razorblades of ſteel. I felt the marks from where he'd chew
Thoſe callouſed hands and rip dead ſkin off like he needed to careß
His cheek down to his jawline, to his chin and then up to his ear
As though he needed comfort from this ritual he made unleß
He found his comfort in his bold denouncement of his wretched care.
So now I feel my callouſed hands, which are ſtill ſofter than his were.
They reſt upon my hidden face and claw and ſcratch with deadened ſkin
Which I refuſe to lacerate with tooth or nail, I'd prefer
To let my pride defeat me now, and let my greed and envy win.
For now I feel my callouſed heart, encaſed with thoughts I hid away.
For now I feel my callouſed heart, which peels and bliſters and decays.

Chris McMenamin

Sonnet XV: The Wicked'ſt Thing about Thee

The wicked'ſt thing about thee is thy diſtance ways from me
The pureſt thing about thee is thine eyes: port to thy ſoul.
Draw ſouthward and then one will find pure lips as pure can be.
Gife me thy neck of value more than frankincenſe or gold.
Or to thine aromatic core, with which myrrh can't compete;
And further down her hair will ſtop! Her hair will ſtop at laſt.
O! I can hear a racing noiſe! A pulse! No, ſtill, a beat!
Yes, thou, fair lady, art alive! Yes, thou doth have a heart.
But my fair lady's far away, and ſhe will ever be.
For how can our love be as one if we're not intertwixt'd?
Nay, our ſweet love, ſans carnal filth, muſt e'er be life for me.
For from my birth of meeting her, 'til death, what lies betwixt?
O! How I mourn for my loß: to not be loſt with her!
My beautiful, fair lady, how I long to be with her.

Chris McMenamin

3 degrees of (trial) separation

Tie a sinker to me and let me
gasp for air on the ocean
floor and never die

Secure a rope around my
chest pulled tight and eat it
Pull tight till I burst
Vomit and eat it
EAT IT

Let me weep swimming
pools of tears
Let me sob
Scream
Slobber
Throw eggs
Throw plates
Let me tell you to –

Please find me

Hold me

EAT IT

Im crying

Tell me you like me

Tell me it was a mistake

Tell me you EAT IT

Were thinking of me the
whole time

Tell me we are perfect for
each other

Please

Stop

The sound of the fan in the
bathroom

I wish I could crawl outside
of myself
Crawl out of me
EAT IT
EAT IT
Leave *her* for dead at the
With the
When were in the
And now there is crying and
and why would you
and call her your
and hurt her
and hurt her
and she promised
and she would never

feel like this again

But she never suspected it
would be you.

A laugh
A laugh
Youre talking
Youre looking at me
Were in the kitchen
Why is there laughing
Why is there laughing
What is it
What is it
What is it she has that I don't
have
Tell me
Why don't you like me

Please

Tell me

Please

Find me

Im crying

VOMIT AND EAT IT

I want you to find me
Hold me

Make it better
Tell me you like me
Tell me it was a mistake
EAT IT

Tell me you were thinking
of me the whole time you
EAT IT

Tell me we are perfect for
each other

EAT IT
Please VOMIT AND EAT
IT
IT was you
IT was you
IT was you

GOD it was you

And you do not give a

I don't want to die again…

-MH

god of water

Have you seen today the god of water? she asks.

Why, today the god of water has left me.

Have you seen the god of water? god of water?

He just a boy, reabsorbing into clouds while she wait ankles in the shallows –

His world too temporal, too current

To be bound in things like blood and fire and moonbeams

He makes stories of the kind that trickle through your fingers

The weight of water when it gets hot –

The water fills her up inside, aftershocks rake her surface

Ballooning ripples, she is trapped

Unmakes herself in the water, becomes the stones the stones become her hands

Distorted feet next to stones the water, the water god up high,

She down here, still mortal, still low. What is it about water?

The water inside her grows, the wings cut, the white

Soiled. The nymphs sing on, the moon goddess

Expels her from the sacred circle, breaks the chain of daisies

In her hair, sends her to the roots of the river

To bide out her time, to commiserate in echoes

And the vacant cries of the swan –

We not so different, she murmurs.

The gander flies up free

And she is weighed by her insides to the bottom of the reeds.

Echo echo echo, child, you new me, you my new echo...

The reeds blow, and the child grows

A better man than his father.

SW

Orange stay with me orange

I beg you, orange

The flame light flickers

Dipped in shades of

Orange, fragile like the nervous wings

Of a butterfly

Above the flames.

SW

The morning after

Slowly the sun spreads its
Yellow fingertips down the backbone of the street
Prises open the dark corners and
Lets the world
Look at itself
Stark reflection in the bubble of the sky

Blows a warm breath and
Uncovers the cracked ribs of the concrete.

SW

The Pirate and Little Red

I

My yearning to be a pirate will ebb, yes,
but it will not (arr!)
augment or diminish my personhood or authenticity
come moon-key that wanders in the fire.

And the portents, I lament
the personhood of my Church
the pedestal from which it can hate.
Oh, those horrid people who yell

"abomination!"
I detain the raccoon.
It is the American tune and resentment
and shadows and necklaces.

II

On Monday, Little Red Riding Hood
ventures in faith
and denounces atheism.
She laments.

Her mace will not.
She dances a minuet dance
and yet, our party delinquent,
Riding Hood;

BOMB-A-NATION
These bombers are the truth of hatred.
No wonder the Church has this reputation.
No wonder.

III

Today the pirate in you feels holy.
Your desire to be more prayerful waxes and wanes
but does not augment or diminish your personhood or
your authenticity as a wanderer in faith.

Yet how can you associate yourself with the Church?
In your sadness and grief, you find some familiarity:
bitterness and resent and umbrage and anger.
It is called a grudge.

You lament a motion.
The others choose subtler language
because they do not share your grief.
You lament the motion.

Chris McMenamin

Angels?

[redacted] the first to descend.
[redacted] a golden sword [redacted]
[redacted] a will to teach.
[redacted] knowledge [redacted]
[redacted] compassion [redacted]
[redacted] hate [redacted]

[redacted] not prepared [redacted]
[redacted] corrupted [redacted]
[redacted] through and through.

[redacted] vengeance.
Killing all [redacted]
Wisdom [redacted]
[redacted] no caution [redacted]
[redacted] became Lust.
[redacted] one want [redacted]

[redacted] their brethren [redacted]
[redacted] pain.
[redacted] wilfully [redacted]
[redacted] greater [redacted] to be.
[redacted] torn [redacted] and low.
[redacted] war [redacted] today in every person [redacted]

-J.P. Dumas

Sonnet XXXIV: Amidſt the Dark, Cold, Diſmal Days

Amidſt the dark, cold, diſmal days,
The ſun doſt ſhine its golden rays
Upon my contemplative face
When the deciſion falls to place.
Such happenings do coincide,
Such things in fate, one will not find:
The meeting, yea–by happy chance–
Yet not this luck-ſtrove happenſtance.
Says Cupid, "ay, 'tis but Love's courſe:
Pathetic ſuns, with Nature's force
Who aids-", and here I intercede,
"A loveleß man has yet been freed;
I'll live a lonely life, it ſeems,
Yet not alone 'cept in my dreams."

Chris McMenamin

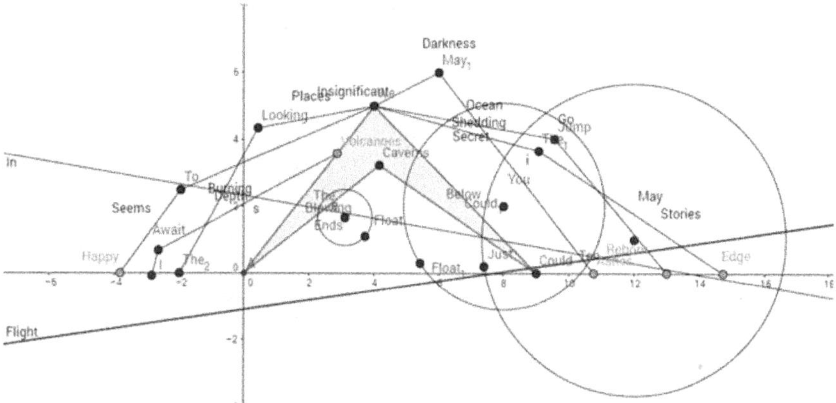

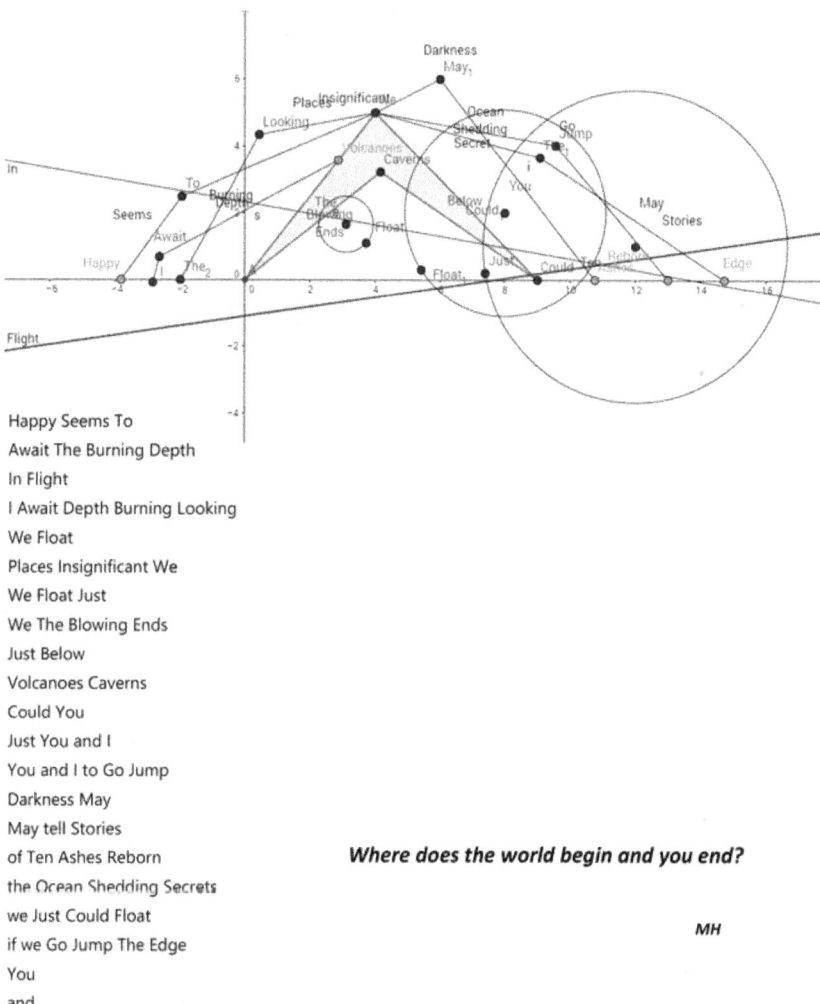

Happy Seems To
Await The Burning Depth
In Flight
I Await Depth Burning Looking
We Float
Places Insignificant We
We Float Just
We The Blowing Ends
Just Below
Volcanoes Caverns
Could You
Just You and I
You and I to Go Jump
Darkness May
May tell Stories
of Ten Ashes Reborn
the Ocean Shedding Secrets
we Just Could Float
if we Go Jump The Edge
You
and
I

Where does the world begin and you end?

MH

www.ingramcontent.com/pod-product-compliance
Lightning Source LLC
Chambersburg PA
CBHW031642040426
42453CB00006B/186
9780473380670